ADVANCE PRAISE FOR
TO TEACH: THE JOURNEY, IN COMICS

BILL AYERS' THEORIES ABOUT TEACHING REFORM REST ON AT LEAST TWO FOUNDATIONS. ONE IS THAT THE HIERARCHICAL RELATIONSHIP BETWEEN THE STUDENT AND TEACHER SHOULD BE MOVED OUT OF THE WAY, FOLLOWED BY SIMULTANEOUS LEARNING BY TEACHER AND STUDENT. THE SECOND IS TO DEMONSTRATE HOW SOME SUBJECTS BLEND WITH OTHERS (MATH WITH SCIENCE) AND ALL SHOULD BE TAUGHT WITH THEIR RELATIONSHIP IN MIND.

SOUNDS GOOD TO ME. A SERIOUS BOOK, BUT LACED WITH HUMOR. IT WILL STRIKE MOST READERS AS A NOVEL APPROACH. REQUIRED READING FOR ALL EDUCATORS.

— HARVEY PEKAR, AUTHOR, *AMERICAN SPLENDOR* SERIES

THIS BOOK IS A TREASURE CHEST OF INSIGHT. IT REPRESENTS WHAT DEDICATED, IMAGINATIVE TEACHING IS ALL ABOUT AND IS A BLUEPRINT FOR EVERYONE WHO WANTS TO EXPLORE THE INTIMATE CONNECTION BETWEEN TEACHING AND LEARNING. BILL AYERS' THOUGHTFUL TEXT IS ILLUMINATED BY RYAN ALEXANDER-TANNER'S PICTURE-PERFECT CARTOONS, CREATING AN ADDED DIMENSION OF WIT AND WISDOM THAT BRINGS COMICS ANOTHER STEP FORWARD IN THEIR EVOLUTION.

— PETER KUPER, CARTOONIST AND EDUCATOR, BOOKS INCLUDE *STICKS AND STONES, DIARIO DE OAXACA,* AND AN ADAPTATION OF KAFKA'S *THE METAMORPHOSIS*

THE PERENNIAL DANCE OF LEARNING THAT CAN ALSO BE TEACHING AT ITS BEST IS BOTH BRILLIANTLY AND GRAPHICALLY SHOWN HEREIN BY MESSRS. AYERS AND ALEXANDER-TANNER. DO KEEP IN MIND THAT ALTHOUGH THEY CAN SHOW YOU THE RIGHT STEPS, YOU STILL HAVE TO LISTEN CLOSELY TO YOUR INTERIOR MUSIC AND FOLLOW ITS CHANGING MELODIES AND RHYTHMS.

— GARY DUMM, ARTIST, *EGO & HUBRIS: THE MICHAEL MALICE STORY,* AND *AMERICAN SPLENDOR*

TO TEACH REPRESENTS A FRESH BREEZE IN THE EDUCATIONAL AND SOCIAL SCIENCE RESEARCH COMMUNITY. IT TAKES DARING TO RECONCEPTUALIZE ENTRENCHED PRACTICES AND TRADITIONAL MODES OF RESEARCH. BUT IT IS BETTER TO FIND NEW SEAS UPON WHICH TO SAIL, THAN OLD PORTS AT WHICH TO DOCK. BILL AYERS AND RYAN ALEXANDER-TANNER HAVE PROVIDED A GLIMPSE OF THAT NEW SEA AND FOR THIS WE SHOULD BE GRATEFUL.

—ELLIOT EISNER, LEE JACKS PROFESSOR EMERITUS AND PROFESSOR EMERITUS OF ART, STANFORD UNIVERSITY

TO TEACH IS GREAT READING NOT ONLY TO STUDENT TEACHERS BUT TO ANYONE WHO HAS A VESTED INTEREST IN OUR EDUCATION SYSTEM. I ESPECIALLY APPRECIATED THE SMACK DOWN OF THE DEHUMANIZING TREND TO PIGEONHOLE EVERY OTHER KID WITH SOME KIND OF "AT RISK" SYNDROME! IT ALSO IS A GREAT EXAMPLE OF HOW COMIC ART IS A VERY EFFICIENT WAY TO COMMUNICATE COMPLEX IDEAS.

—**PETER BAGGE**, COMICS JOURNALIST AND AUTHOR OF THE *BUDDY BRADLEY* SERIES

WEAVING IN INSPIRATIONAL ANECDOTES AND PLAYFUL VISUAL METAPHORS, *TO TEACH: THE JOURNEY, IN COMICS* TAKES US THROUGH ONE SCHOOL YEAR WITH A DELIGHTFUL GROUP OF YOUNG LEARNERS. IN THE PROCESS, AYERS AND ALEXANDER-TANNER'S COLLABORATION CLEVERLY ILLUSTRATES THE VITAL IMPORTANCE—AND MORAL NECESSITY—OF TEACHING.

—**JOSH NEUFELD** WRITER/ARTIST OF *A.D.: NEW ORLEANS AFTER THE DELUGE*

AYERS ORGANIZES A CLASSROOM LIKE ALEXANDER-TANNER LAYS OUT EACH PAGE: WITH INVENTIVENESS, CLARITY OF PURPOSE, AND A CLOSE ATTENTION HONORING THEIR INDIVIDUAL SUBJECTS. I WISH I'D READ THIS BOOK BEFORE I STARTED TEACHING AND MAKING COMICS A DECADE AGO; IT'S CHOCK FULL OF PRACTICAL AND PHILOSOPHICAL ADVICE. AYERS SAYS YOU'RE NOT THERE TO ENTERTAIN OR *SAVE* THE STUDENTS. TEACHING IS PRIMARILY A CHALLENGING AND HUMBLING ACT OF LOVE. EACH STUDENT MUST BE VALUED AS AN INDIVIDUAL RATHER THAN A STATISTIC. KNOWLEDGE IS A TWO-WAY STREET BETWEEN TEACHER AND STUDENT, AND WHEN EVERYTHING WORKS ALL THE INDIVIDUAL VOICES COME TOGETHER TO ENRICH OUR COMMUNITIES. I KNOW THIS BOOK WILL INSPIRE A GENERATION OF TEACHERS TO COME.

—**LAUREN WEINSTEIN**, CARTOONIST AND TEACHER, WRITER/ARTIST, *GIRL STORIES*

TO TEACH IS HILARIOUS SERIOUS AND FABULOUS! A BROAD MANIFESTO THAT WILL CHANGE MANY PEOPLE'S LIVES.

—**LAURIE ANDERSON**, ARTIST AND MUSICIAN

TO TEACH

the journey, in comics

TO TEACH
the journey, in comics

WILLIAM AYERS
RYAN ALEXANDER-TANNER

FOREWORD BY JONATHAN KOZOL

TEACHERS COLLEGE, COLUMBIA UNIVERSITY
NEW YORK AND LONDON

PUBLISHED BY TEACHERS COLLEGE PRESS, 1234 AMSTERDAM AVENUE, NEW YORK, NY 10027

LIBRARY OF CONGRESS CATALOGING-IN-PUBLICATION DATA

AYERS, WILLIAM, 1944—
    TO TEACH: THE JOURNEY, IN COMICS/ WILLIAM AYERS, RYAN ALEXANDER-TANNER;
FOREWORD BY JONATHAN KOZOL.
    p. cm.
INCLUDES BIBLIOGRAPHICAL REFERENCES.
ISBN 978-0-8077-5062-9 (ALK. PAPER)
    1. TEACHING — COMIC BOOKS, STRIPS, ETC. 2. TEACHERS — COMIC BOOKS, STRIPS, ETC.
I. ALEXANDER-TANNER, RYAN. II. TITLE.
LB1025.3.A935   2010
371.102 — dc22   2009075351

ISBN 978-0-8077-5062-9 (PAPER)

PRINTED ON ACID-FREE PAPER
MANUFACTURED IN THE UNITED STATES OF AMERICA

TO DALIN ALEXI AND LIGHT AYLI,
AND FUTURE GENERATIONS OF
COMIC BOOK LOVERS

– BILL

TO ROBIN LINNETT

–RYAN

CONTENTS

FOREWORD

BILL AYERS, OVER THE PAST 30 YEARS, HAS STEADILY EMERGED AS ONE OF THE MOST SENSITIVE AND RESPECTED EDUCATORS IN AMERICA. HIS ACADEMIC WRITINGS HAVE, HOWEVER, YET TO REACH MORE THAN A FRACTION OF THE AUDIENCE THEY DESERVE. NOW, IN COLLABORATION WITH A MARVELOUS CARTOONIST, HE HAS CREATED AN UTTERLY ORIGINAL AND DELICIOUSLY IRREVERENT BOOK THAT IS LIKELY TO BE PASSED FROM HAND TO HAND BY TENS OF THOUSANDS OF OUR NATION'S TEACHERS OUT OF THE SHEER JOY THAT THEY WILL TAKE IN READING IT.

WORDS AND PICTURES, WHEN COMMINGLED WITH A SKILLFUL ARTISTRY, LEAD, IN AYERS'S NICELY CHOSEN WORDS, TO "A DAZZLING DANCE OF THE DIALECTIC" THAT PROPELS US INTO ASKING QUESTIONS WE HAVE NEVER ASKED BEFORE; AND, SPEAKING AS HE DOES IN OFTEN THE SAME PICARESQUE AND VIVID LANGUAGE CHILDREN USE, HE KEEPS THE PAGES OF THIS BOOK ELECTRIC IN THEIR FRESHNESS AND VITALITY.

"MYTHS," HE WRITES, "TOWER ABOVE THE WORLD OF TEACHING LIKE GIANT, FIRE-BREATHING DRAGONS." NOT THE LEAST AMONG THOSE DRAGONS IS THE NOTION THAT "TECHNIQUE" ALONE — AND ESPECIALLY THE TECHNICAL DEVICES TYPICALLY ASSOCIATED WITH A SET OF ARBITRARY STATE-MANDATED STANDARDS THAT INDUCE SUBORDINATION IN THE MINDS OF STUDENTS — ARE A GOOD AND PROPER SUBSTITUTE FOR THE LEARNING THAT ORIGINATES IN THE HEARTS OF CHILDREN AND THE EXHILARATION THAT GOOD TEACHERS TAKE IN PLUNGING "INTO THE UNKNOWN" BESIDE THEM.

"GOODBYE," HE WRITES, "TO COMMAND AND CONQUER... WELCOME TO A CLASSROOM WHERE INSTRUCTION... OVERFLOWS WITH LOVE."

SOME OF THE MOST MEMORABLE CHARACTERS WITHIN THIS SWIFTLY MOVING STORY ARE LIVELY LITTLE BOYS LIKE QUINN, A "DYNAMO" WHO LIVES LIFE AT "FULL TILT" BUT, UNDER THE CURRENTLY OBSESSIVE WISH TO CLASSIFY OUR KIDS IN BOXES THAT HAVE LABELS, WOULD RUN THE RISK IN MANY SCHOOLS THESE DAYS OF BEING TERMED A "HYPERACTIVE CHILD" WHO NEEDS TO BE COOLED OFF IN WHAT ARE ALL TOO OMINOUSLY DESCRIBED AS "SPECIAL SERVICES."

TEACHERS SWEEP INTO THE BOOK AS WELL, LIKE THE FASCINATING ALICE JEFFERSON, WHO DOES A STUDY WITH HER 4TH-GRADE CHILDREN EVERY YEAR ON SOMETHING "SHE KNOWS NOTHING ABOUT" AND IN WHICH HER ENERGY REMAINS AT FEVER PITCH BECAUSE SHE IS AS EAGER AS THE CHILDREN TO COME OUT OF IT WITH INTELLECTUALLY REWARDING ANSWERS.

THE ENFORCERS OF THE STANDARDS, WITH THEIR EVER-PRESENT CLIP-BOARDS, WANDER THROUGH THE TALE LIKE IRRITATING MINOR CHARACTERS IN BATMAN. "MR. AYERS... WE'RE CONCERNED THAT YOU TEACH YOUR STUDENTS TO MEET THE STATE REQUIREMENTS... WE'VE PROVIDED A CONVENIENT OUTLINE OF STATE GUIDELINES FOR YOU." ONE OF THE KIDS ASKS HIM, "HEY, BILL?" ARE THOSE PEOPLE WITH THE CLIPBOARDS COMING BACK?" AND, IN A COMMENT THAT ABOUT 3 MILLION TEACHERS PROBABLY WOULD LOVE TO SAY IF ONLY THEY HAD THE NERVE, THE CHILD ADDS, "THEY'RE WEIRD."

BUT AYERS IS MERCIFUL WITH THE ENFORCERS — "THE CURRICULUM COPS," AS A TEACHER FRIEND OF MINE IN THE SOUTH BRONX DESCRIBES THEM. HE KNOWS THAT MANY ARE INTELLIGENT AND VITAL HUMAN BEINGS WHO ARE CAUGHT UP IN THE SAME RIGIDIFYING ETHOS THAT INTIMIDATES THE CLASSROOM TEACHERS, TOO.

NOR, BLESSEDLY, DOES AYERS ALLOW HIMSELF TO FALL INTO THE SAND-TRAP OF ABSURDITY, SEEN SO FREQUENTLY IN THE INTELLECTUALLY CHAOTIC "FREE SCHOOLS" OF SOME 40 YEARS AGO, WHICH, BY THEIR UTTER AIMLESSNESS, BROUGHT GRAVE DISCREDIT TO THE VALUES OF PROGRESSIVE EDUCATION. ("DON'T WORRY, MRS. JONES," I USED TO HEAR THESE TEACHERS SAY, "WHEN YOUR 10-YEAR-OLD FEELS AN ORGANIC AND SPONTANEOUS DESIRE TO LEARN TO READ, SHE'LL LET US KNOW" — THE KINDS OF WORDS THAT SENT BLACK PARENTS, IN PARTICULAR, RACING FROM THIS ABDICATION OF ADULT RESPONSIBILITY INTO THE OPPOSITE EXTREME AND SET US UP FOR THE REACTIONARY TENETS THAT HAVE NOW BEEN CRYSTALLIZED IN NO CHILD LEFT BEHIND.)

AYERS DOES NOT BELIEVE IN ADULT ABDICATION. "GOOD SCHOOLS," AS HE CITES A TEACHER IN CHICAGO, "ARE PLACES WHERE EDUCATION IS UNDERSTOOD TO BE A MATTER OF LIFE AND DEATH," BUT THEY ARE ALSO PLACES WHERE IT'S OKAY TO BE GOOFY, TO ADMIT TO CHILDREN WHAT ONE DOES NOT KNOW AND WHAT, OFTEN, NO ONE ON THIS EARTH CAN KNOW, THEN TO JOIN THEM IN THE GREAT ADVENTURE OF SEARCHING FOR A RESOLUTION OF THESE MYSTERIES TOGETHER.

HERE'S WHAT I HAVE TO SAY ABOUT THIS LARGELY AUTOBIOGRAPHICAL DELIGHT: "SUPER-GOOD! LOTS OF MISCHIEF! LOTS OF GRIT AND GUTS AND FUN! ZAP! BAM! GADZOOKS! HOORAY!"

Jonathan Kozol ☺

ACKNOWLEDGMENTS

TO MY DAZZLING STUDENTS AT THE UNIVERSITY OF ILLINOIS AT CHICAGO, WHO SCHOOL ME IN THOUSANDS OF WAYS, AGAIN AND AGAIN; TO BERNARDINE AND OUR KIDS, WHO BELIEVED IN AND PUSHED THIS BOOK FORWARD FROM THE START; TO OUR COMRADES IN ARC; TO MAXINE FOR HER CONTINUING INSPIRATION; TO THE INCOMPARABLE CAROLE SALTZ AND HER BRILLIANT AND DEVOTED STAFF, AND ESPECIALLY TO MEG LEMKE FOR HER DEFT AND BRILLIANT INTERVENTIONS—ALL THANKS TO YOU.

—BILL

IT'S OFTEN SAID THAT IT TAKES A VILLAGE TO RAISE A COMIC BOOK, AND THIS ONE WAS CERTAINLY NO EXCEPTION.

THANKS TO BERNARDINE DOHRN FOR HER NURTURING NATURE AND UNPARALLELED TOLERANCE TOWARD 2 GIGGLING BOYS.

TO MEG LEMKE FOR WHIPPING US INTO SHAPE WITH HER GIANT BRAIN, AND TO THE REST OF OUR FRIENDS AT TCP: CAROLE, BEV, EMILY, KARL, PETER, AND SNOOP DAVEY DAVE.

TO IVAN BRUNETTI FOR GENEROUS FEEDBACK AT A CRUCIAL STAGE.

TO PRODUCTION ASSISTANTS SABRINA ABDULLAH AND KIRA KUPFERSBERGER FOR VOLUNTEERING TO SAVE MY LIFE.

TO ALL MY HOMIES WHO SHARED STUDIO TIME: FAREL DALRYMPLE, SCOTT MILLS, ROB G., CATHERINE PEACH, SOPHIE LINNETT, MIA NOLTING, DEVIN CHALMERS, AUGUST LIPP, AND NEIL BRIDEU.

TO ROBERT KATZ AND KAREN ZAMPA-KATZ FOR LAWN GUYLAND HOSPITALITY, AND SCOTT LEON FOR BEING VERY HELPFUL.

TO THE OLD-SCHOOL CREW, MISHA BALMER AND BEN WILKINS-MALLOY.

TO THE TEACHERS WHO TAUGHT ME WHAT GOT ME HERE: EMILY GINSBERG, DANIEL DUFORD, KURT HOLLOMAN, ELI ALEXANDER-TANNER, AND MARK BAUMGARTEN.

TO THIS BOOK'S EXTENDED FAMILY, SONIA ABRAMS, RICK AYERS, JUAN CHICAGO, AND JUDI MINTER, FOR A MILLION THINGS, AND KATIE ROSE LEON FOR BACKRUBS AND MORAL SUPPORT.

AND A SPECIAL THANKS FOR THIS BOOK AND ALL BOOKS BEFORE AND AFTER TO ALEXIS ALEXANDER, SEAMUS HEFFERNAN, AND ALEX CAHILL, A GREATER SUPPORT NETWORK THAN I EVER COULD HAVE HOPED FOR. THANK YOU.

—RYAN

ACKNOWLEDGMENTS

TO MY DAZZLING STUDENTS AT THE UNIVERSITY OF ILLINOIS AT CHICAGO, WHO SCHOOL ME IN THOUSANDS OF WAYS, AGAIN AND AGAIN; TO BERNARDINE AND OUR KIDS, WHO BELIEVED IN AND PUSHED THIS BOOK FORWARD FROM THE START; TO OUR COMRADES IN ARC; TO MAXINE FOR HER CONTINUING INSPIRATION; TO THE INCOMPARABLE CAROLE SALTZ AND HER BRILLIANT AND DEVOTED STAFF, AND ESPECIALLY TO MEG LEMKE FOR HER DEFT AND BRILLIANT INTERVENTIONS – ALL THANKS TO YOU.

– BILL

IT'S OFTEN SAID THAT IT TAKES A VILLAGE TO RAISE A COMIC BOOK, AND THIS ONE WAS CERTAINLY NO EXCEPTION.

THANKS TO BERNARDINE DOHRN FOR HER NURTURING NATURE AND UNPARALLELED TOLERANCE TOWARD 2 GIGGLING BOYS.

TO MEG LEMKE FOR WHIPPING US INTO SHAPE WITH HER GIANT BRAIN, AND TO THE REST OF OUR FRIENDS AT TCP: CAROLE, BEV, EMILY, KARL, PETER, AND SNOOP DAVEY DAVE.

TO IVAN BRUNETTI FOR GENEROUS FEEDBACK AT A CRUCIAL STAGE.

TO PRODUCTION ASSISTANTS SABRINA ABDULLAH AND KIRA KUPFERSBERGER FOR VOLUNTEERING TO SAVE MY LIFE.

TO ALL MY HOMIES WHO SHARED STUDIO TIME: FAREL DALRYMPLE, SCOTT MILLS, ROB G., CATHERINE PEACH, SOPHIE LINNETT, MIA NOLTING, DEVIN CHALMERS, AUGUST LIPP, AND NEIL BRIDEU.

TO ROBERT KATZ AND KAREN ZAMPA-KATZ FOR LAWN GUYLAND HOSPITALITY, AND SCOTT LEON FOR BEING VERY HELPFUL.

TO THE OLD-SCHOOL CREW, MISHA BALMER AND BEN WILKINS-MALLOY.

TO THE TEACHERS WHO TAUGHT ME WHAT GOT ME HERE: EMILY GINSBERG, DANIEL DUFORD, KURT HOLLOMAN, ELI ALEXANDER-TANNER, AND MARK BAUMGARTEN.

TO THIS BOOK'S EXTENDED FAMILY, SONIA ABRAMS, RICK AYERS, JUAN CHICAGO, AND JUDI MINTER, FOR A MILLION THINGS, AND KATIE ROSE LEON FOR BACKRUBS AND MORAL SUPPORT.

AND A SPECIAL THANKS FOR THIS BOOK AND ALL BOOKS BEFORE AND AFTER TO ALEXIS ALEXANDER, SEAMUS HEFFERNAN, AND ALEX CAHILL, A GREATER SUPPORT NETWORK THAN I EVER COULD HAVE HOPED FOR. THANK YOU.

– RYAN

INTRODUCTION: WELCOME TO OUR COMIC BOOK

HOW ABOUT WE START WITH, "BANG! POW! ZOOM! COMICS AREN'T FOR KIDS ANY MORE!"?

ARGH!

WHAT, YOU DON'T LIKE IT? I JUST MADE IT UP...

I'M TELLIN' YOU, BILL... I LOVE COMICS, BUT I'M TIRED OF DEFENDING 'EM.

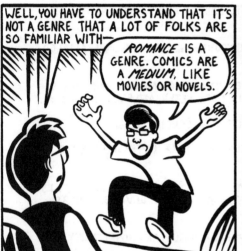

WELL, YOU HAVE TO UNDERSTAND THAT IT'S NOT A GENRE THAT A LOT OF FOLKS ARE SO FAMILIAR WITH—

ROMANCE IS A GENRE. COMICS ARE A MEDIUM, LIKE MOVIES OR NOVELS.

RIGHT, SORRY. I CAN'T IMAGINE WHY MORE PEOPLE DON'T KNOW IT WHEN YOU'RE SO TOLERANT AND INVITING...

I'VE READ COMICS MY WHOLE LIFE, BUT THERE ARE SO MANY ASPECTS TO HOW THEY WORK THAT I NEVER CONSIDERED UNTIL WE SAT DOWN TO WRITE THIS ONE.

YEAH?

I THOUGHT WE WERE SIMPLY COMBINING WORDS WITH PICTURES, BUT THAT MARRIAGE GIVES BIRTH TO A THIRD, ALL-NEW FORM— SEQUENTIAL ART AND A DAZZLING DANCE OF THE DIALECTIC.

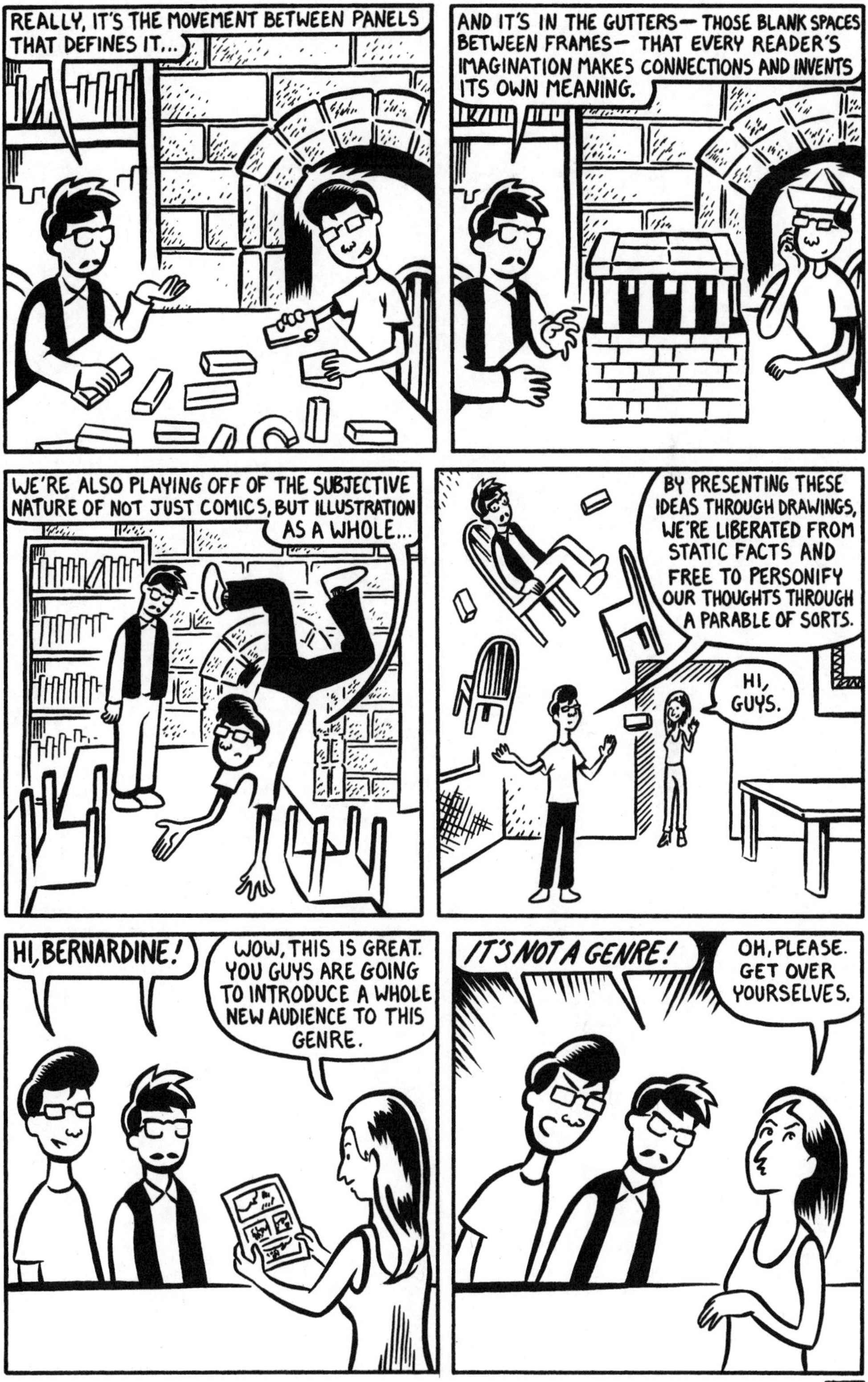
REALLY, IT'S THE MOVEMENT BETWEEN PANELS THAT DEFINES IT...
AND IT'S IN THE GUTTERS— THOSE BLANK SPACES BETWEEN FRAMES— THAT EVERY READER'S IMAGINATION MAKES CONNECTIONS AND INVENTS ITS OWN MEANING.
WE'RE ALSO PLAYING OFF OF THE SUBJECTIVE NATURE OF NOT JUST COMICS, BUT ILLUSTRATION AS A WHOLE...
BY PRESENTING THESE IDEAS THROUGH DRAWINGS, WE'RE LIBERATED FROM STATIC FACTS AND FREE TO PERSONIFY OUR THOUGHTS THROUGH A PARABLE OF SORTS.
HI, GUYS.
HI, BERNARDINE!
WOW, THIS IS GREAT. YOU GUYS ARE GOING TO INTRODUCE A WHOLE NEW AUDIENCE TO THIS GENRE.
IT'S NOT A GENRE!
OH, PLEASE. GET OVER YOURSELVES.

1
OPENING DAY: THE JOURNEY BEGINS

THE WORDS "TEACHING" AND "TEACHER" EVOKE IN ALMOST EVERYONE PARTICULAR MEMORIES AND IMAGES. FOR SOME, THESE MEMORIES ARE DULL, EVEN FEARFUL — THEY INCLUDE BOREDOM, ROUTINE, AND WORSE. FOR THOSE OF US WHO CONSTRUCT LIVES IN TEACHING, THESE IMAGES ARE NECESSARILY CHANGING AND GROWING, AND WHILE THEY ARE SOMETIMES VIVID AND CONCRETE, THEY CAN AS OFTEN BE CHARACTERIZED BY WONDER. IN EITHER CASE, IMAGES OF TEACHING CAN FILL US WITH AWE, AND WE CAN CHOOSE TO SEE WITHIN THEM AN ABIDING SENSE OF ADVENTURE AND CHALLENGE.

WHEN I BEGAN TEACHING — ON THE FIRST MORNING OF MY VERY FIRST KINDERGARTEN CLASS...

WHY DOES THE BALL BOUNCE?

AHH...

OH, FIGS! I DON'T EVEN KNOW *THAT!*

BEFORE I KNEW IT, I WAS STRUGGLING JUST TO KEEP MY HEAD ABOVE WATER.

WHY IS THE SKY BLUE?

WHY?

WHY DID MY DAD HAVE TO GO TO WAR?

WHY?

WHY?

WHY IS YOUR SKIN PINK AND MY SKIN BROWN?

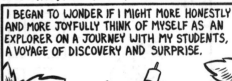

THIS WAS MY FIRST CRISIS. WHAT IS TEACHING, AND WHO IS A TEACHER?

MUST THE TEACHER ALWAYS BE THE MASTER AND COMMANDER OF THE SHIP, POISED WITH COMPLETE CONFIDENCE, IN CHARGE AND IN CONTROL?

I BEGAN TO WONDER IF I MIGHT MORE HONESTLY AND MORE JOYFULLY THINK OF MYSELF AS AN EXPLORER ON A JOURNEY WITH MY STUDENTS, A VOYAGE OF DISCOVERY AND SURPRISE.

HOWEVER, THE EXPLORER APPROACH IS EASIER SAID THAN DONE.

ON THIS ODYSSEY, THE TEACHER MUST ANTICIPATE AN EPIC, SOLITARY QUEST.

I FOUND MYSELF NAVIGATING TURBULENT WATERS, STRUGGLING TO OVERCOME A SEEMINGLY ENDLESS SEA OF DANGEROUS OBSTACLES ALONG THE WAY.

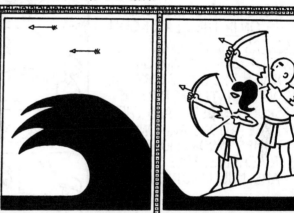

UNLIKE THE HEROES OF LEGEND, THE TEACHER TRUDGES TOWARD AN UNCERTAIN FUTURE WITHOUT EASY REWARDS.

IN FACT, IT'S OFTEN THE MYTHS THEMSELVES THAT THE YOUNG TEACHER MUST FIGHT AGAINST.

3

POPULAR MYTHS ABOUT TEACHING

KIDS TODAY ARE WORSE THAN EVER BEFORE

IT'S TRUE! JUST ASK MY CONTEMPORARIES, SOCRATES AND SHAKESPEARE:

THE CHILDREN NOW LOVE LUXURY. THEY HAVE BAD MANNERS, CONTEMPT FOR AUTHORITY... THEY CONTRADICT THEIR PARENTS, GOBBLE DOWN FOOD AT THE TABLE, AND INTIMIDATE THEIR TEACHERS.

I WOULD THAT THERE WERE NO AGE BETWEEN 10 AND 3 AND 20 — OR THAT BOY WOULD SIMPLY SLEEP OUT THE REST, FOR THERE IS NOTHING IN THE BETWEEN BUT WRONGING THE ANCESTRY, STEALING AND FIGHTING.

TEACHERS ALWAYS KNOW WHAT'S GOING ON IN THE CLASSROOM

TEACHERS ALWAYS KNOW ONE STORY OF WHAT'S GOING ON, AND IT'S NEVER THE ONLY STORY. KIDS ARE ACTIVE INTERPRETERS OF CLASSROOM REALITY AND THEIR INTERPRETATIONS ARE ONLY SOMETIMES SYNONYMOUS WITH THE TEACHER'S. TRUE STORIES ARE MULTITUDINOUS.

THE TEACHER'S WORK IS TO "SAVE" THE CHILDREN

"CHILD-SAVING" HAS A SAD AND TROUBLED HISTORY, FILLED WITH GOOD INTENTIONS BUT ALSO PATRONIZATION AND GLIB ASSUMPTIONS ABOUT FAMILIES AND COMMUNITIES. CHILDREN NEED TO BE VALUED AND SUPPORTED, LOVED AND ENCOURAGED, NOURISHED AND CHALLENGED. LEAVE THE "SAVING" AT THE DOOR. TEACH.

GOOD TEACHERS ARE GOOD PERFORMERS

SOMETIMES...BUT GOOD TEACHERS DO NOT ROUTINELY CLAIM "CENTER STAGE." THAT SPOT IS RESERVED FOR THEIR STUDENTS. GOOD TEACHERS AREN'T "FUN." FUN IS AMUSING AND DIVERTING. LEARNING CAN BE ENGROSSING, AMAZING, DISORIENTING, TRANSPORTING — AND IF IT'S JOYFUL OR DELIGHTFUL, EVEN BETTER.

ALL CHILDREN ARE ABOVE AVERAGE

THIS IS THE "MYTH OF THE 3RD GRADE": "SHE'S READING AT THE 3RD-GRADE LEVEL." IT'S AS IF THERE'S AN IDEAL 3RD-GRADER ON MOUNT OLYMPUS. EVERY 4TH-GRADE TEACHER IS ANGRY AT EVERY 3RD-GRADE TEACHER— MOST KIDS DON'T ARRIVE "ON LEVEL" OR "READY." THE TRUTH IS 3RD-GRADERS ARE VARIOUS, AND GOOD TEACHERS TEACH TO THAT DIVERSITY.

GOOD TEACHERS ALWAYS KNOW THE MATERIAL

SURE, THAT'S WHY TEACHERS ARE ALWAYS READING, WONDERING, EXPLORING, COLLECTING, GOING TO THE MOVIES OR MUSEUMS OR CONCERTS OR LECTURES AND EXPOSITIONS; WE CAN'T GET ENOUGH. BUT THE UNIVERSE IS EXPANDING, AND KNOWLEDGE IS INFINITE. AT SOME POINT, GOOD TEACHERS MUST PLUNGE INTO THE UNKNOWN ALONGSIDE THEIR STUDENTS, TO ADVENTURE ON TOGETHER.

NOW LET'S TAKE A LOOK AT A COUPLE OF REAL-LIFE SITUATIONS...

STARTING WITH JOSÉ LA LUZ, A FORMER STUDENT OF MINE.

SCHOOL FAILURE FIT JOSÉ AND FOLLOWED HIM LIKE A SHADOW. HE MISBEHAVED SO OFTEN THAT THE PATH TO THE PRINCIPAL'S OFFICE BECAME A RUT HE WALKED MANY TIMES.

MY STRUGGLE WAS TO FIND SOMETHING JOSÉ VALUED THAT WE MIGHT BUILD UPON. IN MARCH I SAW A KNOT OF KIDS SKATEBOARDING OVER AND AROUND SOME HUGE DRAIN PIPES AT A CONSTRUCTION SITE NEAR SCHOOL, AND IN THE MIDDLE OF IT ALL, KING OF THE MOUNTAIN, WAS JOSÉ.

KEEP OUT

CONSTRUCTION ZONE

I ASKED JOSÉ SOME DAYS LATER IF HE COULD TEACH A MINICOURSE ON SKATEBOARDING TO THE CLASS. HE AGREED.

PROVIDING A SPACE FOR JOSÉ'S PASSION AND EXPERTISE ALLOWED HIM TO BRING HIS OWN WISDOM INTO THE ROOM. THE RESULT WASN'T A SUDDEN OR PERFECT TURNAROUND, BUT IT WAS A START.

TEACHERS MIGHT EXAMINE THEIR OWN INTERESTS IN SEARCH OF A CONNECTION...

PAUL UNDERHILL IS A 4TH-GRADE TEACHER, FRESH OUT OF GRAD SCHOOL.

HE SEES TEACHING AS A NOBLE PROFESSION, AND DREAMS HIS CLASSROOM CAN BECOME A POSITIVE, SUPPORTIVE EDUCATIONAL COMMUNITY.

HIS IDEALS CLASH REGULARLY WITH REALITY—CLASSROOM MANAGEMENT ALONE IS AN OVERWHELMING CHALLENGE.

HE DOES SO MUCH, AND YET FEELS ONLY THE WEIGHT OF WHAT REMAINS TO BE DONE. TEACHING OCCUPIES HIM DAY AND NIGHT.

ONE PLACE HE FINDS SOLACE IS A WEEKLY ELECTIVE OF HIS OWN INVENTION. "THE LYRICISTS LOUNGE" IS A CREATIVE WRITING ACTIVITY WHERE KIDS RHYME AND PERFORM ORIGINAL COMPOSITIONS:

♪ GRANDMAS, THEY GIVE YOU MONEY AND THEY'RE THE ONES WHO CALL YOU HONEY THEY LAUGH AND SMILE 'CAUSE THEY'RE SO FUNNY AND THEY KEEP THE FOOD INSIDE MY TUMMY ♪

PAUL'S PASSION MEETS THE KIDS' INTERESTS IN AN IMAGINATIVE COMMON GROUND, THE FOUNDATION FOR CREATING A PRODUCTIVE CLASSROOM. PAUL'S JOURNEY IS JUST BEGINNING...

BUT SKATEBOARDS AND RAPPING SOLVE *ALL* YOUR CLASSROOM PROBLEMS ONLY IN THE MOVIES. I ENJOY A TRIP TO THE CINEMA AS MUCH AS ANYONE, BUT PROJECTING SILVER SCREEN MYTHS ON TO OUR STUDENTS OBSCURES THE PATH TO DISCOVERY. IN ORDER TO FIND YOUR WAY, YOU MUST TURN THE PROJECTOR AROUND AND SEARCH WITHIN.

MYTHS TOWER ABOVE THE WORLD OF TEACHING LIKE GIANT, FIRE-BREATHING DRAGONS. SOMEHOW TEACHERS NEED TO SLAY THESE CREATURES IN ORDER TO MOVE FROM MYTH TO REALITY.

AND THE REALITIES CAN BE HARSH. I CAN THINK OF A MILLION REASONS NOT TO TEACH JUST OFF THE TOP OF MY HEAD...

TEACHERS ARE BADLY PAID, SO BADLY THAT IT'S A NATIONAL DISGRACE. THERE IS NO OTHER PROFESSION THAT DEMANDS SO MUCH AND RECEIVES SO LITTLE IN COMPENSATION.

EXCEPT FOR "COMICS ARTIST."

TEACHERS OFTEN WORK IN DIFFICULT SITUATIONS UNDER IMPOSSIBLE CIRCUMSTANCES, WITH TOO MANY KIDS, TOO LITTLE TIME, STINGY RESOURCES, AND HEARTLESS BUREAUCRATS PEERING THROUGH THE DOOR.

TEACHERS SUFFER LOW STATUS IN SOCIETY, IN PART AS A LEGACY OF SEXISM. TEACHING IS LARGELY WOMEN'S WORK, AND IT IS CONSTANTLY BEING DESKILLED, MADE INTO SOMETHING TO BE PERFORMED MECHANICALLY, COVERED OVER WITH LAYERS OF SUPERVISION AND ACCOUNTABILITY, AND HELD IN LOW ESTEEM.

AND THAT'S BARELY THE START OF IT! THE LIST COULD GO ON AND ON...

IN SPITE OF ALL OF THIS, THE WORLD OF TEACHING CAN BE DEEPLY SATISFYING.

THERE ARE STILL CHILDREN AND YOUTH WHO NEED THOUGHTFUL AND CARING ADULTS IN THEIR LIVES — MENTORS WHO CAN UNDERSTAND AND GUIDE THEM.

AND OUR COMMUNITIES AND COUNTRY ARE STILL IN NEED OF RENEWAL AND REPAIR.

THERE ARE ALWAYS SPECIFIC, INDIVIDUAL WORLDS TO BE CHANGED, ONE BY ONE.

TO NAME ONESELF AS A TEACHER IS TO LIVE WITH ONE FOOT IN THE MUCK OF THE WORLD AS WE FIND IT — WITH ITS CONVENTIONAL PATTERNS AND RECEIVED WISDOM — AND THE OTHER FOOT STRIDING TOWARD A WORLD THAT COULD BE BUT ISN'T YET.

EVEN THE MOST COMMITTED, CARING TEACHERS WILL MAKE MISTAKES ALONG THE WAY, BUT THEY WON'T BE DISASTROUS.

TEACHING AT ITS BEST IS NOT A MATTER OF TECHNIQUE — IT'S PRIMARILY AN ACT OF LOVE.

11

GOODBYE TO COMMAND AND CONQUER. GOODBYE TO A TRIVIAL PURSUIT OF THE OBVIOUS. GOODBYE TO EASY, UNSATISFYING ANSWERS.

WELCOME TO THE HARD WORK OF TEACHING TOWARD A BETTER WORLD. WELCOME TO A CLASSROOM WHERE INSTRUCTION JUMPS OFF THE PAGE AND OVERFLOWS WITH LOVE. WELCOME TO LEARNING AS AN ACT OF CONSTRUCTION AND RECONSTRUCTION.

WELCOME   BIENVENIDO

2
SEEING THE STUDENT

TEACHING IS AN INTERACTIVE PRACTICE THAT BEGINS AND ENDS WITH SEEING THE STUDENT. IT IS ONGOING AND NEVER COMPLETELY FINISHED. THE STUDENT GROWS AND CHANGES, THE TEACHER LEARNS, THE SITUATION SHIFTS, AND SEEING BECOMES AN EVOLVING CHALLENGE. AS LAYERS OF MYSTIFICATION AND OBFUSCATION ARE PEELED AWAY, AS THE STUDENT BECOMES MORE FULLY PRESENT TO THE TEACHER, EXPERIENCES AND WAYS OF THINKING AND KNOWING THAT WERE INITIALLY OBSCURE BECOME THE GROUND ON WHICH AN AUTHENTIC AND VITAL TEACHING PRACTICE CAN BE CONSTRUCTED.

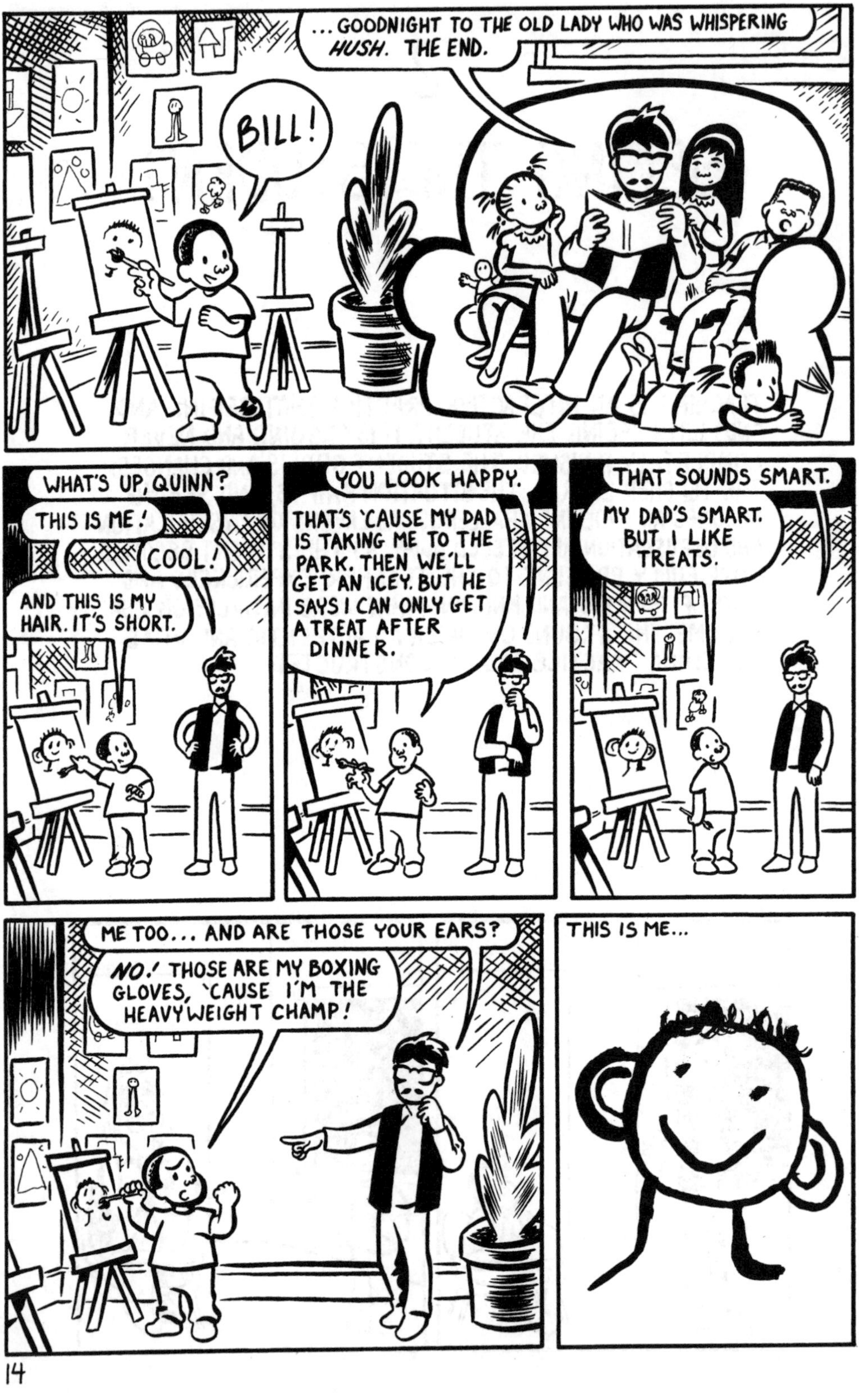
...GOODNIGHT TO THE OLD LADY WHO WAS WHISPERING *HUSH*. THE END.
BILL!
WHAT'S UP, QUINN?
THIS IS ME!
COOL!
AND THIS IS MY HAIR. IT'S SHORT.
YOU LOOK HAPPY.
THAT'S 'CAUSE MY DAD IS TAKING ME TO THE PARK. THEN WE'LL GET AN ICEY. BUT HE SAYS I CAN ONLY GET A TREAT AFTER DINNER.
THAT SOUNDS SMART.
MY DAD'S SMART. BUT I LIKE TREATS.
ME TOO... AND ARE THOSE YOUR EARS?
NO! THOSE ARE MY BOXING GLOVES, 'CAUSE I'M THE HEAVYWEIGHT CHAMP!
THIS IS ME...

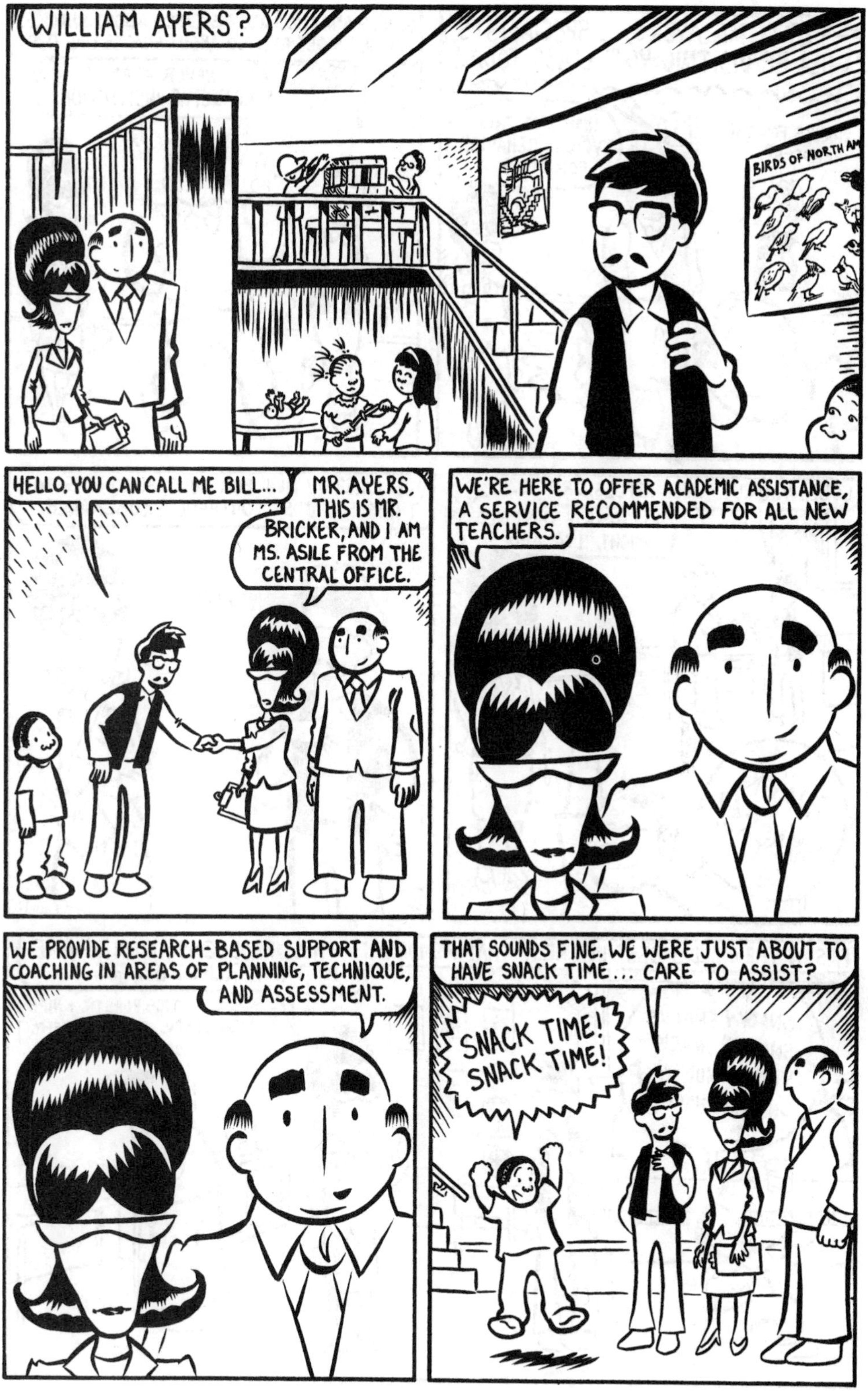
WILLIAM AYERS?
BIRDS OF NORTH AM
HELLO. YOU CAN CALL ME BILL...
MR. AYERS, THIS IS MR. BRICKER, AND I AM MS. ASILE FROM THE CENTRAL OFFICE.
WE'RE HERE TO OFFER ACADEMIC ASSISTANCE, A SERVICE RECOMMENDED FOR ALL NEW TEACHERS.
WE PROVIDE RESEARCH-BASED SUPPORT AND COACHING IN AREAS OF PLANNING, TECHNIQUE, AND ASSESSMENT.
THAT SOUNDS FINE. WE WERE JUST ABOUT TO HAVE SNACK TIME... CARE TO ASSIST?
SNACK TIME! SNACK TIME!

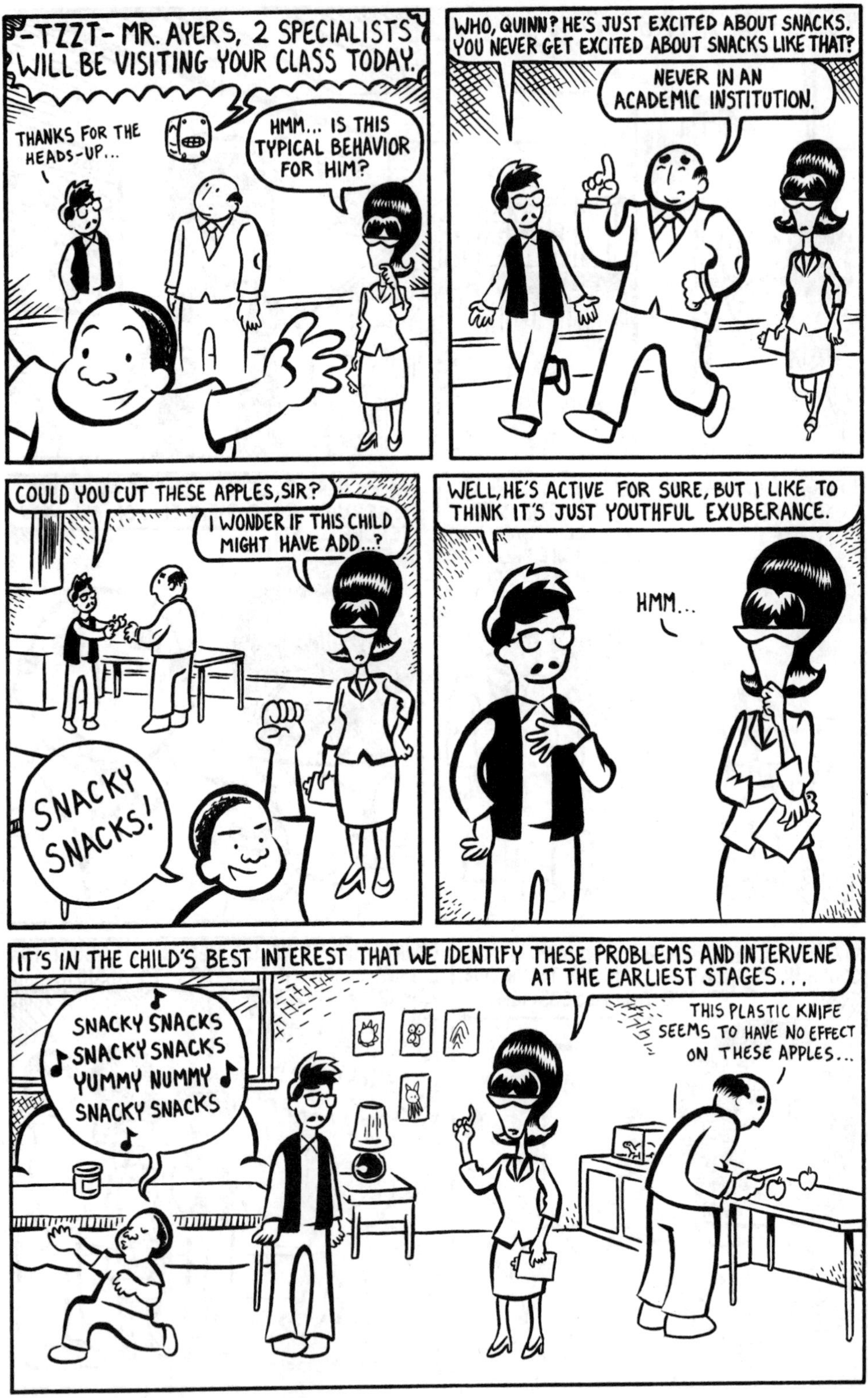
-TZZT- MR. AYERS, 2 SPECIALISTS WILL BE VISITING YOUR CLASS TODAY.
THANKS FOR THE HEADS-UP...
HMM... IS THIS TYPICAL BEHAVIOR FOR HIM?
WHO, QUINN? HE'S JUST EXCITED ABOUT SNACKS. YOU NEVER GET EXCITED ABOUT SNACKS LIKE THAT?
NEVER IN AN ACADEMIC INSTITUTION.
COULD YOU CUT THESE APPLES, SIR?
I WONDER IF THIS CHILD MIGHT HAVE ADD...?
SNACKY SNACKS!
WELL, HE'S ACTIVE FOR SURE, BUT I LIKE TO THINK IT'S JUST YOUTHFUL EXUBERANCE.
HMM...
IT'S IN THE CHILD'S BEST INTEREST THAT WE IDENTIFY THESE PROBLEMS AND INTERVENE AT THE EARLIEST STAGES...
SNACKY SNACKS SNACKY SNACKS YUMMY NUMMY SNACKY SNACKS
THIS PLASTIC KNIFE SEEMS TO HAVE NO EFFECT ON THESE APPLES...

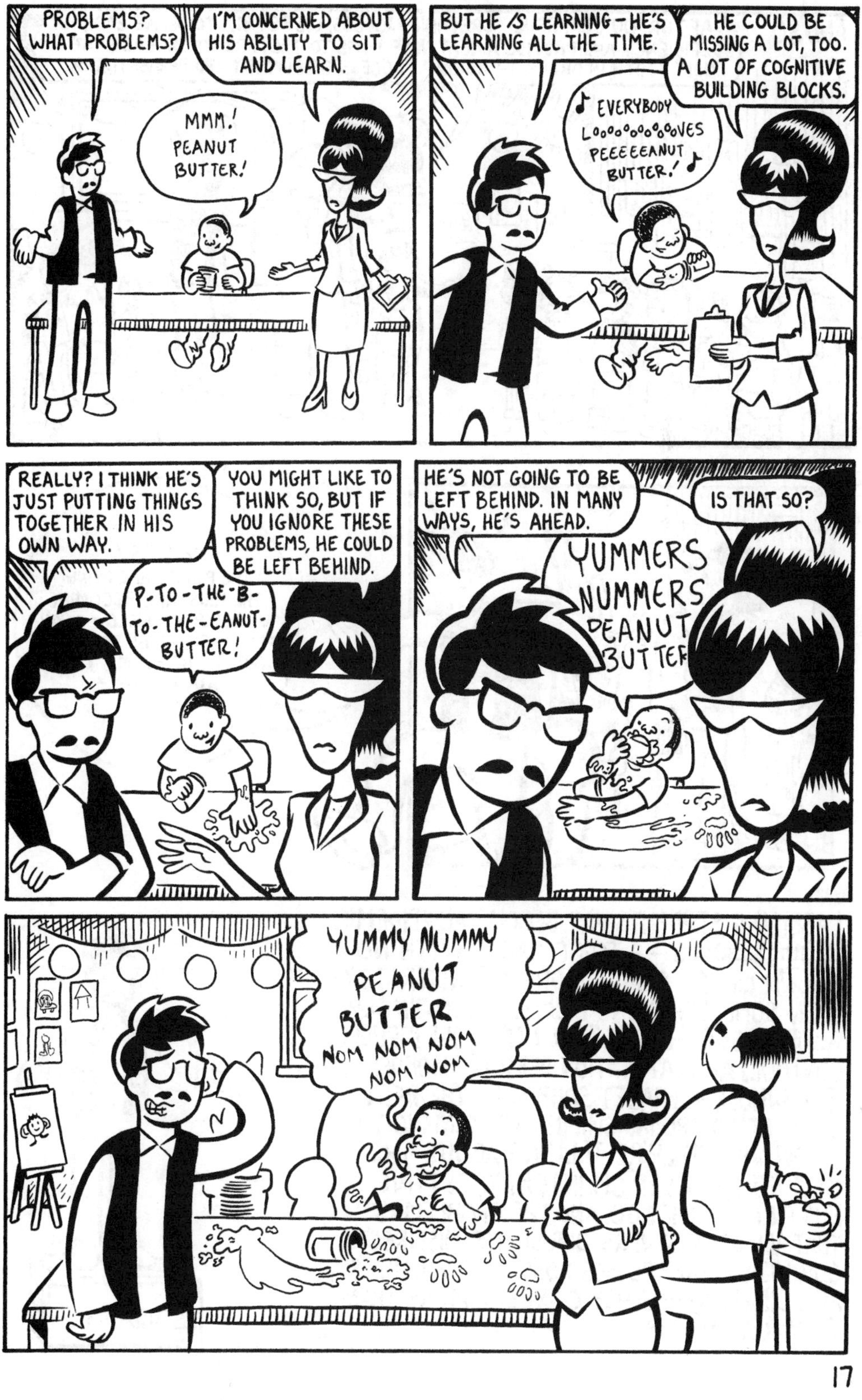
PROBLEMS? WHAT PROBLEMS?
I'M CONCERNED ABOUT HIS ABILITY TO SIT AND LEARN.
MMM! PEANUT BUTTER!
BUT HE IS LEARNING—HE'S LEARNING ALL THE TIME.
HE COULD BE MISSING A LOT, TOO. A LOT OF COGNITIVE BUILDING BLOCKS.
♪ EVERYBODY LOOOOOOOOOOVES PEEEEEANUT BUTTER! ♪
REALLY? I THINK HE'S JUST PUTTING THINGS TOGETHER IN HIS OWN WAY.
YOU MIGHT LIKE TO THINK SO, BUT IF YOU IGNORE THESE PROBLEMS, HE COULD BE LEFT BEHIND.
P-TO-THE-B-TO-THE-EANUT-BUTTER!
HE'S NOT GOING TO BE LEFT BEHIND. IN MANY WAYS, HE'S AHEAD.
IS THAT SO?
YUMMERS NUMMERS PEANUT BUTTER
YUMMY NUMMY PEANUT BUTTER NOM NOM NOM NOM NOM

LABELLING STUDENTS HAS BECOME AN EPIDEMIC IN OUR SCHOOLS — A TOXIC HABIT WITH NO KNOWN LIMITS. SUPERVISORS, ADMINISTRATORS, EVEN SOME TEACHERS MUMBLE KNOWINGLY ABOUT "SOFT SIGNS" OR **LIC** (LOW IMPULSE CONTROL), ADD (ATTENTION DEFICIT DISORDER)... THE WHOLE ALPHABET SOUP... AND THE REST OF US STAND AROUND SMILING, PRETENDING TO KNOW WHAT THEY'RE TALKING ABOUT. THE CATEGORIES KEEP SPLINTERING, GETTING NUTTIER AS THEY GO, AND THE PROBLEM IS THAT ALL OF IT LOWERS OUR SIGHTS, MISDIRECTS OUR VISION, SUPPRESSES POSSIBILITY. LABELS ARE LIMITING — THEY CONCEAL MORE THAN THEY REVEAL.

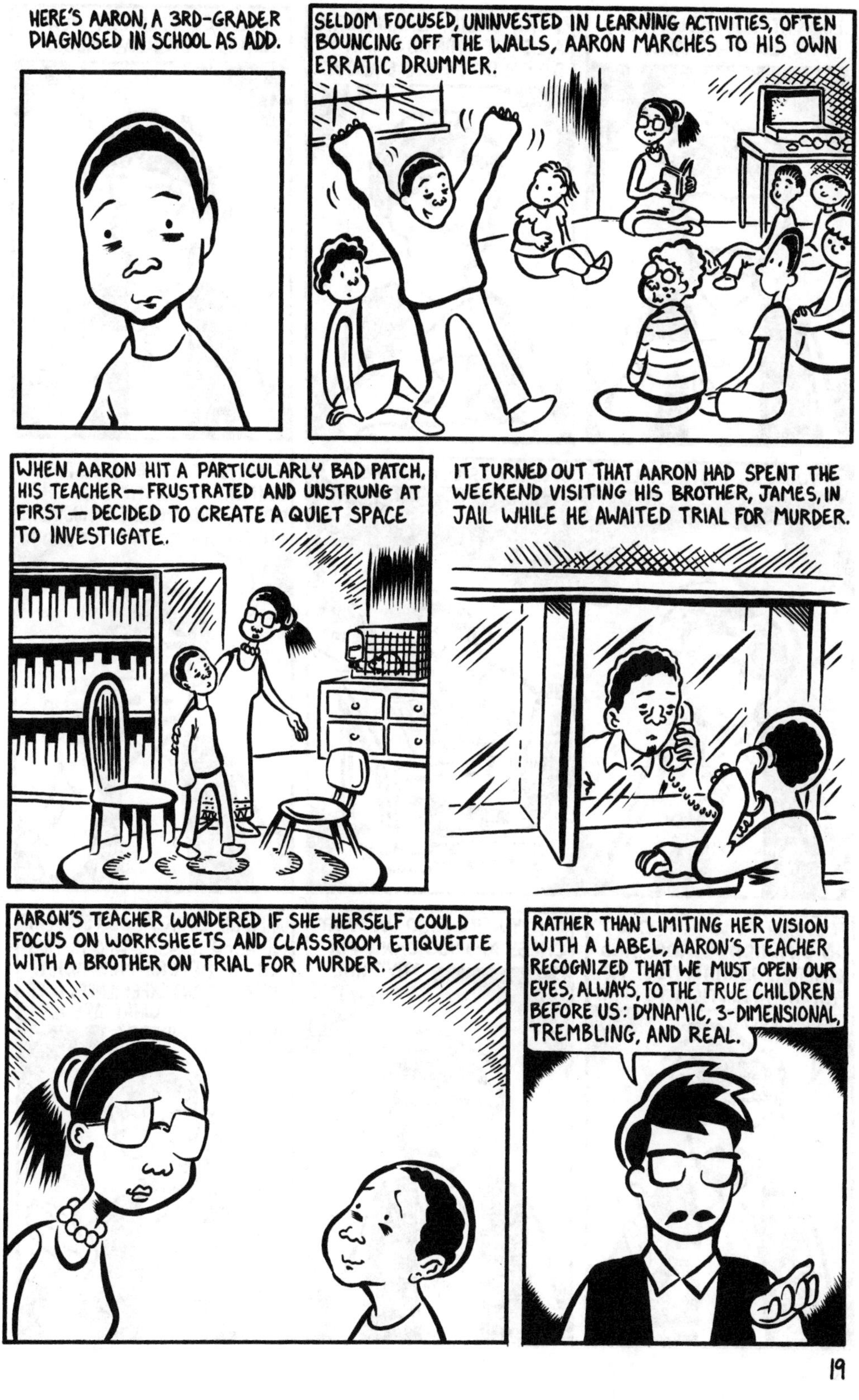
HERE'S AARON, A 3RD-GRADER DIAGNOSED IN SCHOOL AS ADD.
SELDOM FOCUSED, UNINVESTED IN LEARNING ACTIVITIES, OFTEN BOUNCING OFF THE WALLS, AARON MARCHES TO HIS OWN ERRATIC DRUMMER.
WHEN AARON HIT A PARTICULARLY BAD PATCH, HIS TEACHER—FRUSTRATED AND UNSTRUNG AT FIRST—DECIDED TO CREATE A QUIET SPACE TO INVESTIGATE.
IT TURNED OUT THAT AARON HAD SPENT THE WEEKEND VISITING HIS BROTHER, JAMES, IN JAIL WHILE HE AWAITED TRIAL FOR MURDER.
AARON'S TEACHER WONDERED IF SHE HERSELF COULD FOCUS ON WORKSHEETS AND CLASSROOM ETIQUETTE WITH A BROTHER ON TRIAL FOR MURDER.
RATHER THAN LIMITING HER VISION WITH A LABEL, AARON'S TEACHER RECOGNIZED THAT WE MUST OPEN OUR EYES, ALWAYS, TO THE TRUE CHILDREN BEFORE US: DYNAMIC, 3-DIMENSIONAL, TREMBLING, AND REAL.

LOOK AT YOURSELF...OR, HECK, LOOK AT ME...

I CAN EASILY BRAINSTORM A LIST OF THINGS I CAN'T DO OR DON'T CARE ABOUT...

LET'S SEE...I CAN'T PLAY TENNIS...OR READ MUSIC...

YOU CAN'T SIT STILL... YOU CAN'T CARRY A TUNE...

RIGHT, BUT... I'VE AN ASTUTE CRITICAL AESTHETIC FOR THE MOVIES, AND I'M AN ENTHUSIASTIC CHEF.

FOCUSING ON WHAT I *CAN'T* DO DIMINISHES HOPE AND LIMITS POSSIBILITIES. IT PAYS NO ATTENTION TO WHAT I *CAN* DO.

OH! YOU'RE ALSO LOUSY AT CHESS AND YOU CAN'T FIX ANYTHING!

C'MON, WE'RE PAST THAT NOW...

WHEN WE LOOK AT OUR STUDENTS WE NEED TO ASK, "WHO IS THIS PERSON BEFORE ME? WHAT INTERESTS AND EXPERIENCES DOES SHE BRING? WHAT ARE HIS AREAS OF WONDER?"

LABELS ARE LAZY, STATIC. TAKE THE STEREOTYPE DU JOUR, THE TRENDY AND EVER USEFUL "AT RISK."

EVERYONE USES IT, BUT NO ONE CAN SAY EXACTLY WHAT IT MEANS. "AT RISK" FUNCTIONS AS A METAPHOR, A KIND OF VOLUNTARY GROUP MADNESS: IF EVERYONE SEES EVIDENCE OF WITCHCRAFT, THERE MUST BE WITCHES.

"AT RISK" ADDS AN AUTHENTICATING MEDICAL DIMENSION TO A PRESCRIPTION MADE LONG BEFORE ANY INVESTIGATION BEGINS.

IT BECOMES, THEN, A TOTALIZING AND PERSISTENT STEREOTYPE THAT CONFINES PERSPECTIVE AND DEFIES OUR PATIENT SEARCH FOR THE WHOLE CHILD.

EACH OF US IS NOT ONLY COMPLEX, DYNAMIC, IN-THE-MIX, AND ON THE MOVE, BUT WE CAN BE CONTRADICTORY BEINGS MINUTE-TO-MINUTE.

"AT RISK" IS SIMPLY NOT A SATISFACTORY SELF-IDENTIFIER. HOW DOES BEING REDUCED TO THIS SIGNATURE IMPACT THE WAY KIDS SEE THEMSELVES?

OUR YOUNGEST SON, CHESA, ARRIVED IN OUR FAMILY WHEN HE WAS 14 MONTHS OLD.

AS HE GREW OLDER, HE BECAME DOWNCAST, DEPRESSED. LATER THIS DEPRESSION GAVE WAY TO EXPLOSIVE ANGER, OFTEN SELF-DIRECTED.

HE WAS CLUMSY, BOTH PHYSICALLY AND SOCIALLY, AND HE WOULD FREQUENTLY CRASH INTO PEOPLE AND EXPERIENCE GENUINE CONFUSION AT THEIR ANGER.

WHEN WE SET OFF TO OUR FIRST PARENT/TEACHER MEETING, WE WERE READY TO DEFEND CHESA AGAINST ANY CRITICISM HIS TEACHER, KEVIN SWEENEY, MIGHT HAVE...

GOOD AFTERNOON...

YOU BOTH KNOW CHESA BETTER THAN I EVER COULD... WHAT CAN YOU TELL ME THAT WOULD MAKE ME A BETTER TEACHER FOR HIM?

WELL... HE'S... GOT KIND OF A TEMPER...

THAT'S *TRUE*... CHESA CAN BE... *CHALLENGING* IN CLASS...

BUT HE CAN ALSO BE EXTREMELY FOCUSED AND HARDWORKING WHEN HE FINDS WORK THAT INTERESTS AND ENGAGES HIM.

THAT WAS TRUE, ALSO. KEVIN SWEENEY SAW BEYOND THE "PROBLEM CHILD" AND RECOGNIZED THAT CHESA HAD A WIDE RANGE OF DIMENSIONS, SOME CHALLENGING, OTHERS MORE HOPEFUL. KEVIN'S CALM CLARITY MADE HIM AN ALLY TO US AND A GUIDE TO CHESA TOWARD HIS OWN FOCUS, STRENGTHS, AND SUCCESS.

WHAT AND WHO DO WE SEE AS WE LOOK OUT AT OUR STUDENTS? A SEA OF UNDIFFERENTIATED FACES? A SET OF IQS AND TEST SCORES? A COLLECTION OF DEFICITS? OR DO WE SEE POTENTIAL?

WHEN ELLA FITZGERALD, THE GREAT JAZZ DIVA, PASSED AWAY, THE TRIBUTE THAT CAUGHT MY EYE NOTED HER TIME IN A YOUTH DETENTION CENTER.

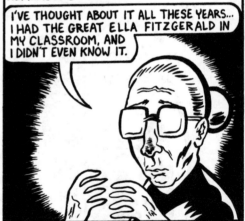

HER ENGLISH TEACHER FROM THOSE DAYS REMEMBERED ELLA...

I'VE THOUGHT ABOUT IT ALL THESE YEARS... I HAD THE GREAT ELLA FITZGERALD IN MY CLASSROOM, AND I DIDN'T EVEN KNOW IT.

THE TRAGEDY IS THAT THEY WERE *ALL* ELLAS, PEOPLE OF WORTH AND POSSIBILITY, AND THE SCHOOL HAD NO WAY TO KNOW IT. AS A TEACHER, I WONDER, WOULD I HAVE MISSED ELLA? COULD I HAVE MADE VISIBLE THE TALENT AND WISDOM IN THE ROOM? HOW?

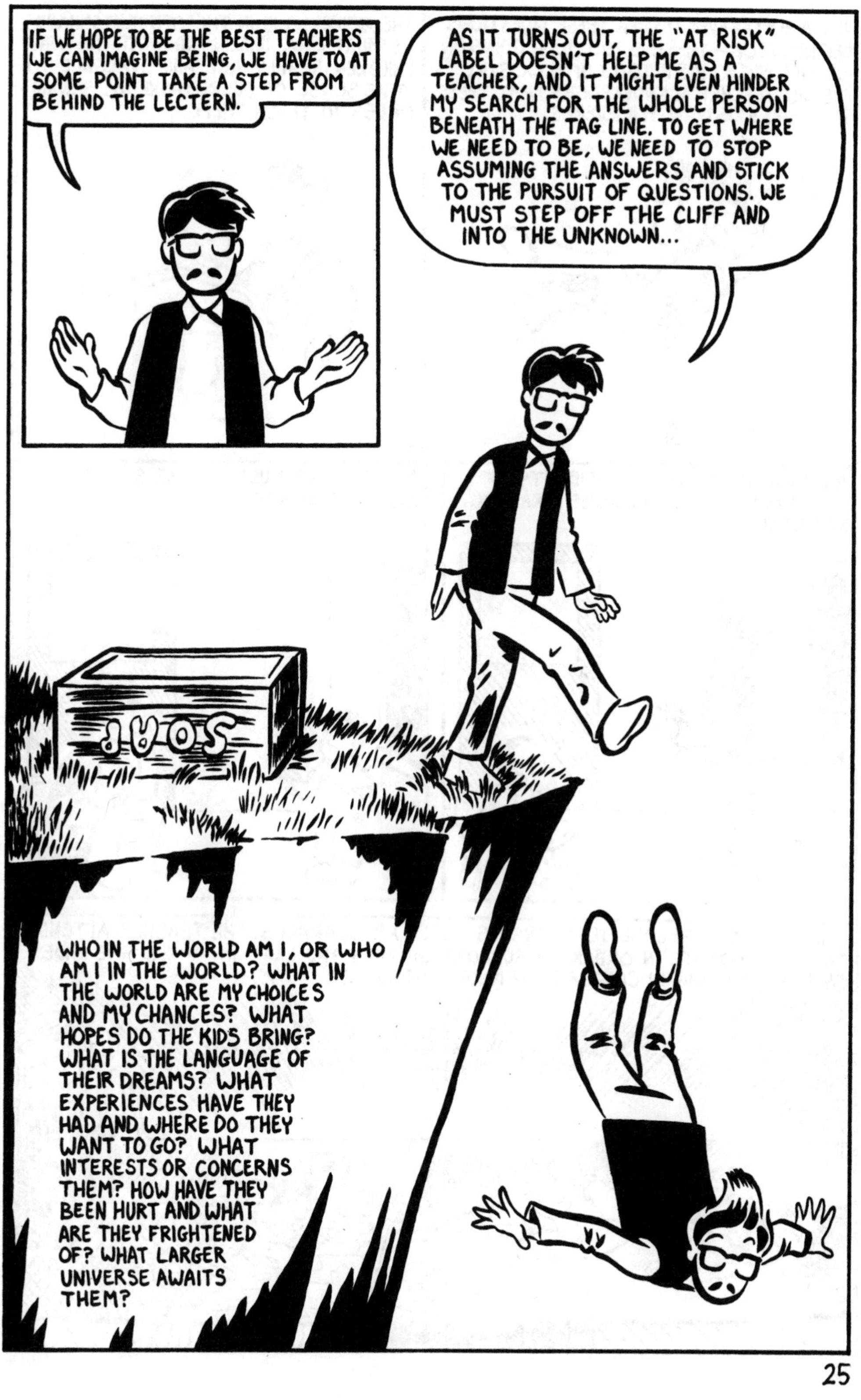
IF WE HOPE TO BE THE BEST TEACHERS WE CAN IMAGINE BEING, WE HAVE TO AT SOME POINT TAKE A STEP FROM BEHIND THE LECTERN.
AS IT TURNS OUT, THE "AT RISK" LABEL DOESN'T HELP ME AS A TEACHER, AND IT MIGHT EVEN HINDER MY SEARCH FOR THE WHOLE PERSON BENEATH THE TAG LINE. TO GET WHERE WE NEED TO BE, WE NEED TO STOP ASSUMING THE ANSWERS AND STICK TO THE PURSUIT OF QUESTIONS. WE MUST STEP OFF THE CLIFF AND INTO THE UNKNOWN...
SOAP
WHO IN THE WORLD AM I, OR WHO AM I IN THE WORLD? WHAT IN THE WORLD ARE MY CHOICES AND MY CHANCES? WHAT HOPES DO THE KIDS BRING? WHAT IS THE LANGUAGE OF THEIR DREAMS? WHAT EXPERIENCES HAVE THEY HAD AND WHERE DO THEY WANT TO GO? WHAT INTERESTS OR CONCERNS THEM? HOW HAVE THEY BEEN HURT AND WHAT ARE THEY FRIGHTENED OF? WHAT LARGER UNIVERSE AWAITS THEM?

NO TEACHER CAN EVER ANSWER THESE QUESTIONS DEFINITIVELY — THERE IS TOO MUCH GOING ON AND *LIFE* IS TOO VAST, TOO COMPLEX. STILL, THE WISE TEACHER ACKNOWLEDGES THAT THESE QUESTIONS EXIST AND PERSEVERES.

THE ANSWERS LIE IN THE STUDENTS' HANDS. WE MUST LOOK UNBLINKINGLY AT THE WAY CHILDREN REALLY ARE AND STRUGGLE TO MAKE SENSE OF EVERYTHING WE SEE IN ORDER TO TEACH THEM.

A COMMITMENT TO THE VISIBILITY OF STUDENTS AS PERSONS REQUIRES A RADICAL REVERSAL:

ALL TEACHERS MUST BECOME STUDENTS OF *THEIR* STUDENTS.

THE STUDENTS BECOME TEACHERS AS WELL AS LEARNERS. THE TEACHER ATTENDS TO THE STUDENTS IN ORDER TO SUPPORT GROWTH AND LEARNING — WE ARE SIDE BY SIDE WORKING IN CONCERT TO KNOW THE WORLD.

WHILE WORKING TOGETHER, WE NEED TO LEARN TO SEE EACH OTHER AS FULLY AS POSSIBLE.

IT'S TOO EASY TO CARICATURE EVERY EXCITABLE AFRICAN-AMERICAN BOY AS "AT RISK." CAREFUL CHILD OBSERVATION IS AN ANTIDOTE TO SUCH SLOPPY THINKING.

A DEVELOPED STUDENT PORTRAIT CAN ONLY EMERGE FROM AN ACCUMULATION OF OBSERVATIONS AND WORK SAMPLES, NOTES AND SKETCHES, STUDIES AND ILLUSTRATIONS.

Quinn is a human dynamo in the classroom, living each day full tilt.

He's an enthusiastic participant in activities, the first to join in, the first to make a connection and reach for the next thing.

He often arrives early to class as his Dad drops him off on his way downtown. Quinn bursts through the door and circles the room as his Dad stows lunch and backpack into his cubby.

Quinn convinces his Dad to read to him before heading off to work, a comforting daily routine.

Good morning, Bill.

Hi, how are you?

Dad, let's read a book!

OK, one book and then I have to get to work...

Quinn gets along well with adults and other kids and has an easy rapport with almost everyone.

Show the slightest interest in his work and Quim will explain, demonstrate, offer information and perspective. Ask a simple question and he'll do the rest.

One morning after circle time Quim spent a half-hour creating a massive structure in the block area. His industriousness drew a crowd. Other builders joined in the work and Quim effortlessly transformed into the chief contractor and superintendent.

Make a road there.

Connect it to my bridge.

How's it going?

Ok. This is my fort where we get ready for adventures. This is for animals and here is the heliport.

A heliport?

It's a place helicopters land.

And I live here with my baby and my mom.

Quinn's filled with delightful energy. Sometimes he can become so excited that he can be aggressive, but never with animosity.

One afternoon, rushing to kick a soccer ball, he knocked over Min-Xuan.

He looked stricken as he picked her up, slowing down considerably afterwards.

For the rest of the afternoon he stayed close to Min-Xuan, checking up on her with a concerned look on his face.

ATTENDING TO THE DETAILS OF ONE CHILD CAN STRENGTHEN OUR UNDERSTANDING OF EVERY CHILD. CLOSE OBSERVATION IS NECESSARY IN SETTINGS WHERE STANDARDIZED WAYS OF LOOKING AT KIDS ARE DEEPLY ENTRENCHED.

THE GOAL OF OBSERVATION IS UNDERSTANDING, NOT SOME IMAGINED OBJECTIVITY. PUSHING TO SEE AND UNDERSTAND EACH CHILD IS AN ACT OF COMPASSION, AND A CENTRAL CHALLENGE TO TEACHING WELL.

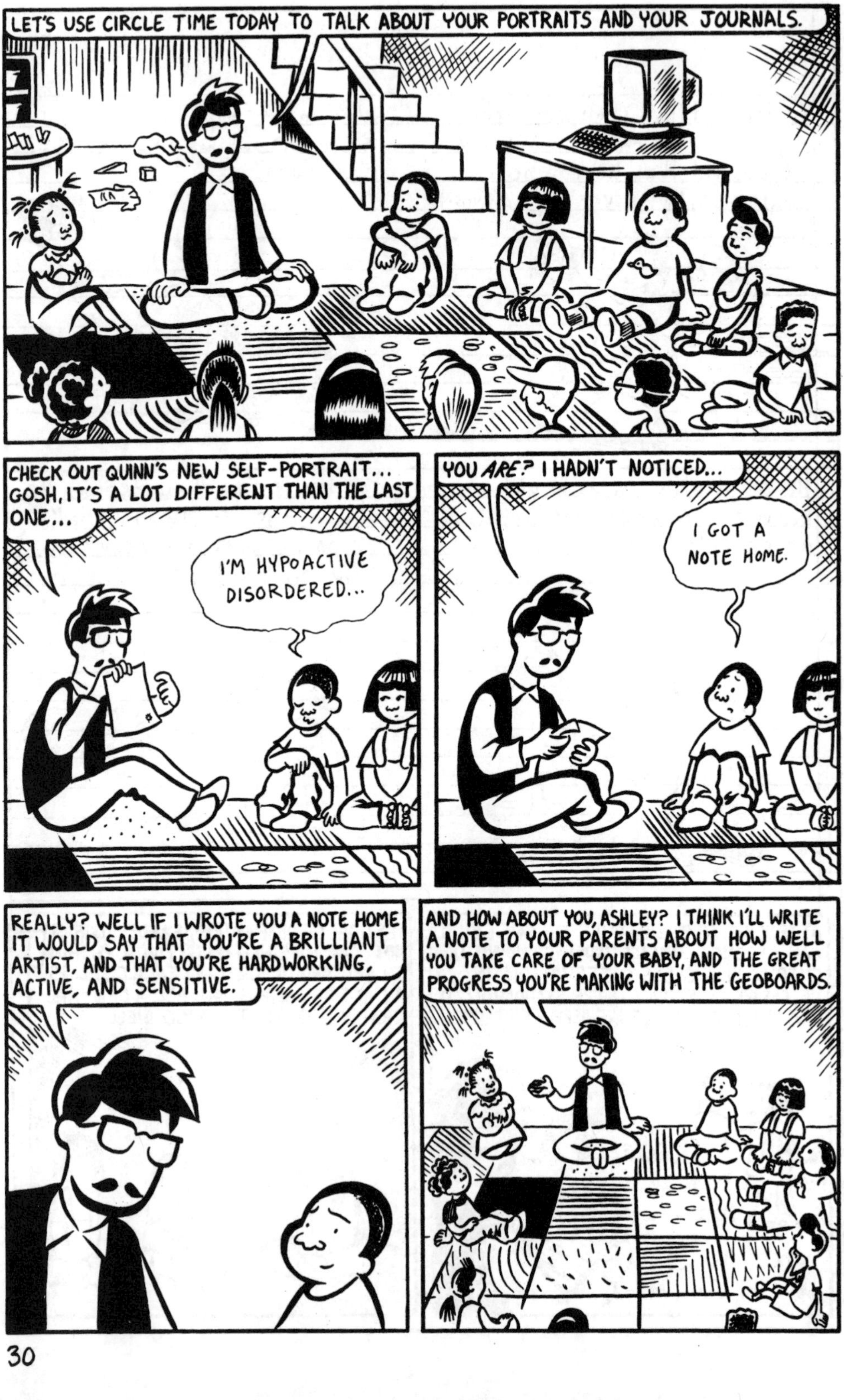

LET'S USE CIRCLE TIME TODAY TO TALK ABOUT YOUR PORTRAITS AND YOUR JOURNALS.
CHECK OUT QUINN'S NEW SELF-PORTRAIT... GOSH, IT'S A LOT DIFFERENT THAN THE LAST ONE...
I'M HYPOACTIVE DISORDERED...
YOU ARE? I HADN'T NOTICED...
I GOT A NOTE HOME.
REALLY? WELL IF I WROTE YOU A NOTE HOME IT WOULD SAY THAT YOU'RE A BRILLIANT ARTIST, AND THAT YOU'RE HARDWORKING, ACTIVE, AND SENSITIVE.
AND HOW ABOUT YOU, ASHLEY? I THINK I'LL WRITE A NOTE TO YOUR PARENTS ABOUT HOW WELL YOU TAKE CARE OF YOUR BABY, AND THE GREAT PROGRESS YOU'RE MAKING WITH THE GEOBOARDS.

GENESIS'S MOM SHOULD KNOW THAT SHE'S THE FASTEST RUNNER, AND THAT SHE ALWAYS HELPS ME CARRY SUPPLIES.

GENESIS SHARED HER CHIPS WITH ME TODAY.

IF I WROTE A NOTE FOR CARL, WHAT WOULD IT SAY?

CARL'S MY BEST FRIEND.

CARL'S A FAST READER.

GREAT! WE ALL HAVE LOTS OF THINGS WE'RE GOOD AT AND OTHER THINGS WE'RE LEARNING TO DO BETTER.

THE CHALLENGE IS TO SEE ONE ANOTHER GENEROUSLY AND WHOLE RATHER THAN BIT BY BEHAVIORAL BIT.

I'M A FIRE-FIGHTER!

I'M A BALLERINA.

I'M AN ASTRONAUT... AND A BASKETBALL PLAYER.

I'M A SAMURAI!

31

THAT'S RIGHT! EACH OF YOU CAN BE ANYTHING YOU WANT, BECAUSE SEEING IS SUBJECTIVE.

WHAT'S THAT?

IT MEANS THE WORLD CAN BE VIEWED AND EXPERIENCED AS YOU LIKE IT.

AND WHEN I LOOK OUT AT EACH AND EVERY ONE OF YOU, I SEE UNRULY SPARKS OF MEANING-MAKING ENERGY ON A VOYAGE OF DISCOVERY THROUGH LIFE. THAT'S THE ONLY LABEL BIG ENOUGH FOR YOU AND EMBRACING ENOUGH FOR THIS ROOM.

HEY, BILL?

YEAH?

ARE THOSE PEOPLE WITH THE CLIPBOARDS COMING BACK?

YEAH, I THINK SO.

THEY'RE WEIRD.

3

CREATING AN ENVIRONMENT FOR LEARNING

A LARGE PART OF THE WORK OF TEACHING IS CONSTRUCTING THE LABORATORY FOR LEARNING. IT MUST BE SUFFICIENTLY BROAD AND VARIED TO CHALLENGE A RANGE OF INTERESTS AND ABILITIES, AND YET FOCUSED ENOUGH TO OFFER STUDENTS SOME COHERENT RHYTHMS AND GOALS. LIFE IN CLASSROOMS, AFTER ALL, IS LIFE ITSELF. THE LEARNING ENVIRONMENT IS A COMPLEX, LIVING REFLECTION OF A TEACHER'S VALUES.

BJ'S CHILDCARE HONORS THE INTENTIONS AND WORK OF TODDLERS. ANYTHING THEY NEED IS AT ARM'S REACH, EVERYTHING FITTED FOR THEIR USE. EACH CHILD FEELS WELCOMED, COMPETENT, AND POWERFUL. THE MESSAGE IS: BE A KID!

AT THIS POPULAR FURNITURE EMPORIUM, THE MESSAGE IS: BUY! BUY! BUY! THE STORE PROVIDES A CONSUMER PATH AND JUST AS THE JOURNEY BECOMES EXHAUSTING, THE CAFETERIA MAGICALLY APPEARS.

THE BAHA'I TEMPLE INVITES CONTEMPLATION AND MEDITATION. IT EMBODIES THE PRINCIPLES OF HARMONY AND BALANCE, PEACE AND ENLIGHTENMENT. THE GOSSAMER DOME ALLOWS AN INFUSION OF LIGHT FROM ALL DIRECTIONS. ALL THAT IS SOLID MELTS INTO AIR.

RYAN WORKS, SLEEPS, EATS, AND WEEPS IN THIS STUDIO. STACKS OF PAPER—REFERENCE IMAGES, WORKS-IN-PROGRESS, WORKS OF ART, EMPTY RAMEN PACKETS—FILL EVERY INCH IN WHAT HE CLAIMS IS AN ELABORATE FILING SYSTEM. THE SPACE CRIES, "I AM A PRISONER OF ART."

WHAT DO WE WANT FROM OUR CLASSROOMS? WHAT VALUES AND PURPOSES CAN WE BUILD INTO OUR ENVIRONMENTS? WHAT MESSAGES DO STUDENTS GET WHEN THEY WALK THROUGH THE DOOR? WHAT DOES THE SPACE INVITE THEM TO DO?

I WONDER ABOUT THE WAY KIDS EXPERIENCE SCHOOL, A PLACE WHERE LEARNING IS LINKED MORE TO AGE THAN ANYTHING ELSE, AND THEIR GROWTH, DEVELOPMENT, AND WISDOM ARE NEATLY DIVIDED INTO 9-MONTH UNITS.

THEY FIGURE OUT THAT KNOWLEDGE IS CUT UP INTO DISCIPLINES, DISCIPLINES INTO SUBJECTS, SUBJECTS INTO UNITS OF STUDY. THE DAY IS BROKEN INTO SHORT PERIODS, EVEN IN THE EARLY GRADES, AND EACH PERIOD IS DEVOTED TO A SPECIFIC SUBJECT.

KIDS DISCOVER THAT ADULTS THINK LEARNING IS BIT BY BIT, AND AFTER 200 DAYS OF SCHOOLING EACH STUDENT WILL HAVE ADDED 200 BITS OF MATH, 200 PIECES OF SCIENCE, 200 SLICES OF LITERATURE, AND SO ON. SUCCESSFUL STUDENTS LEARN TO LINE IT UP.

EVERY FEATURE OF LIFE IN SCHOOL CARRIES MESSAGES: THIS IS HOW PEOPLE LEARN, THIS IS HOW PEOPLE THINK, THIS IS THE NATURE OF KNOWLEDGE, THIS IS WHAT IS VALUABLE. THESE MESSAGES CONSTITUTE A MAJOR PART OF WHAT IS LEARNED IN, AND WHAT BECOMES ASSUMED ABOUT, SCHOOL.

WHY DO CHILDREN CHANGE GRADES EACH YEAR? WHY ARE MATH AND SCIENCE SEPARATE SUBJECTS? WHY ARE CHILDREN LINING UP IN THE HALLWAY? WHY IS THE TEACHER STANDING IN FRONT OF THE CLASS DOING MOST OF THE TALKING, AND THE STUDENTS SITTING AT THEIR DESKS QUIETLY MOST OF TIME?

THE MORE AWARE WE ARE OF OUR THOUGHTS AND OUR GOALS, THE MORE WE QUESTION EVERYTHING, THE MORE RESPONSIBLE WE ARE FOR OUR VALUES AND BELIEFS, THE MORE INTENTIONAL WE CAN BECOME IN CREATING SPACES THAT SPEAK AND WORK FOR US.

HERE IS OUR MIDDLE SON, MALIK, ON HIS FIRST DAY OF 5TH GRADE.

I ALWAYS LIKE TO START THE YEAR BY ESTABLISHING THAT IN MY CLASSROOM, THERE ARE ONLY 3 RULES.

RULE #1: YOU CAN CHEW GUM.

WHOA!

F'REAL?

RULE #2: YOU CAN WEAR HATS.

RAD!

DANG.

NO WAY!

RULE #3: THIS IS A COMMUNITY OF LEARNERS, AND YOU MUST TREAT EVERYONE WITH RESPECT AND COMPASSION — ESPECIALLY WHEN IT'S HARD TO DO.

IN A STRAIGHTFORWARD WAY, THIS TEACHER HAD CREATED A SPACE FOR MORAL REFLECTION AND ETHICAL ACTION. RIGHT AWAY HIS CLASSROOM BECAME A PLACE WHERE LEARNING TO LIVE TOGETHER WAS A HIGH VALUE.

TODAY MALIK IS HIMSELF A TEACHER.

FOR A TIME HE TAUGHT SECOND-LANGUAGE LEARNERS IN A CALIFORNIA HIGH SCHOOL. EACH OF HIS STUDENTS HAD MOUNTAINS TO CLIMB IN TERMS OF VOCABULARY, GRAMMAR, SYNTAX, AND USAGE.

MALIK PROVIDED DAILY STORY-STARTERS THAT PROVOKED DISTINCT NARRATIVES THAT BECAME PERSONAL PRIMERS FOR LANGUAGE LEARNING.

Today "People always ask me."

THE RESPONSES WERE ELECTRIFYING: SHORT STORIES AND PERSONAL ESSAYS, POEMS AND LISTS AND CARTOONS. SOME WERE SERIOUS, SOME EARNEST, OTHERS COMICAL AND FULL OF FANCY. LATER MALIK SPENT TIME WITH EACH STUDENT EDITING, CORRECTING, INSTRUCTING.

MALIK HAD OVER 20 DIFFERENT LANGUAGES IN HIS CLASSROOM. HE ENCOURAGED HIS STUDENTS TO TEACH HIM WORDS, MEANINGS, CUSTOMS.

ARE THERE THINGS I SHOULD KNOW? THINGS I SHOULDN'T DO? THINGS I NEED TO DO BETTER?

MALIK'S ENVIRONMENT HAS ITS OWN BIG MEANINGS: EVERYONE IS AN AUTHOR OF HIS OR HER OWN TEXT. WE ARE EACH AN EXPERT ON OUR OWN LIVES. COME IN, SHARE YOUR STORY!

WHAT WOULD AN ENVIRONMENT BUILT AROUND A DESIRE TO KNOW AND TO BE LOOK LIKE?

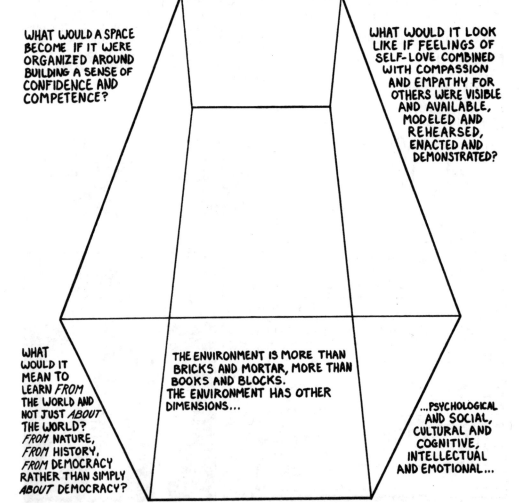

WHAT WOULD A SPACE BECOME IF IT WERE ORGANIZED AROUND BUILDING A SENSE OF CONFIDENCE AND COMPETENCE?

WHAT WOULD IT LOOK LIKE IF FEELINGS OF SELF-LOVE COMBINED WITH COMPASSION AND EMPATHY FOR OTHERS WERE VISIBLE AND AVAILABLE, MODELED AND REHEARSED, ENACTED AND DEMONSTRATED?

WHAT WOULD IT MEAN TO LEARN *FROM* THE WORLD AND NOT JUST *ABOUT* THE WORLD? *FROM* NATURE, *FROM* HISTORY, *FROM* DEMOCRACY RATHER THAN SIMPLY *ABOUT* DEMOCRACY?

THE ENVIRONMENT IS MORE THAN BRICKS AND MORTAR, MORE THAN BOOKS AND BLOCKS.
THE ENVIRONMENT HAS OTHER DIMENSIONS...

...PSYCHOLOGICAL AND SOCIAL, CULTURAL AND COGNITIVE, INTELLECTUAL AND EMOTIONAL...

YOU CAN START WITH SOMETHING SMALL...

FOR EXAMPLE, I CHOOSE TO NOT HAVE A TEACHER'S DESK, AND USE THAT FORMIDABLE SPACE FOR A COMMON WORK TABLE. I DON'T WANT TO HAVE A MINI-LECTURE HALL WITH INERT STUDENTS IN ROWS FACING FRONT. THE MESSAGE IS: LEARNING IS ACTIVE, AND WE'RE ALL IN THIS TOGETHER.

EACH KID IN MY CLASS CHOOSES AN "ICON" TO PUT ON HIS OR HER CUBBY, THE BOARD, THEIR PAINTING, NEXT TO THEIR NAME... THIS IS A NEAT ADDITION TO EARLY LITERACY AND A PERSONALIZED SIGNATURE THAT FOSTERS IDENTITY FORMATION. KIDS MAKE THE LINK BETWEEN A FAMILIAR SYMBOL AND A STABLE DEEPER MEANING — AN ESSENTIAL STEP TOWARD DECODING PRINTED LANGUAGE.

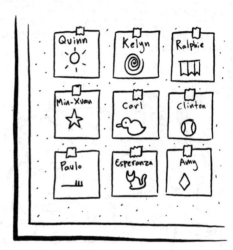

EVEN SEEMINGLY MUNDANE ENVIRONMENTAL CHOICES ARE PACKED WITH MEANING!

BECAUSE LEARNING IS ACTIVE, NOT PASSIVE, I WANT MY CLASSROOM TO BRISTLE WITH ACTIVITY. IT'S OFTEN SAID THAT YOU CAN LEARN SOMETHING FROM ANYTHING. I BELIEVE THAT YOU CAN LEARN *EVERYTHING* FROM *ANYTHING*.

FOR EXAMPLE, COOKING IS A SIMPLE ACTIVITY WITH ENDLESS POSSIBILITY. IN MY CLASSROOM, SOMETHING IS ALWAYS BUBBLING AWAY.

COOL COOKING IS PREPARING FOOD WITHOUT A HEAT SOURCE: FRUIT SALADS, CELERY BOATS, PEANUT BUTTER PLAY-DOH. KIDS COUNT AND MEASURE AND READ AND MIX.

WE MADE AN OVEN OUT OF A CARDBOARD BOX, TIN FOIL, AND LIGHTBULBS, FOR BAKING. THIS INTRODUCED ELEMENTS OF CHEMISTRY AND CONVERSION.

CONNECTIONS EXTEND AND MULTIPLY, OPENING TO FAMILY CULTURE, THEN HISTORY AND GEOGRAPHY. RALPHIE'S MOM BRINGS IN GNOCCHI AND A STORY OF GRANDMA NONA. JENET'S MOM BRINGS IN A ROTI RECIPE AND WE FIND HAITI ON THE MAP.

COOKING IS ENGAGING IN ITS OWN RIGHT, BUT PURSUED EVERY DAY AND FOLLOWED TO ITS LIMIT, WE CAN DISCOVER WORLDS WITHIN WORLDS.

BINGO THE BOX TURTLE WAS OUR CLASS PET.

THE KIDS NAMED HIM AND LOVED TO SING A SONG:

> ♪ I HAD A TURTLE, OH SO FINE
> AND BINGO WAS HIS NAME-O ♪
> B-I-N-G-O, B-I-N-G-O, B-I-N-G-O,
> AND BINGO WAS
> HIS NAME-O ♪

WE HAD TO LOOK AFTER BINGO — TO FEED AND EXERCISE AND CLEAN HIM — AND HE HELPED SET A CARING AND RESPONSIBLE TONE IN THE CLASSROOM.

HE ALSO PROVIDED OPPORTUNITIES FOR OBSERVATION AND RECORD-KEEPING, WRITING AND STORYTELLING.

BINGO'S FOOD CHART

biNGO is
My FreND
today I
WASHed HiM

I KNOW YOU'RE GETTING YOUR HEAD MASHED ALL THE TIME, BINGO, BUT IT'S FOR THE GREATER GOOD.

43

I WANT TO BUILD SPACES WHERE EACH PERSON IS VISIBLE TO ME AND TO EVERYONE ELSE — AND, MOST IMPORTANTLY, TO THEMSELVES. STUDENTS SHOULD SENSE THEIR OWN UNIQUE POWER AND POTENTIAL. IN THIS CLASSROOM, EACH IS KNOWN AND UNDERSTOOD, RECOGNIZED AND VALUED.

I WANT TO BUILD SPACES WHERE THE WISDOM IN THE ROOM IS UNCOVERED AND THE EXPERIENCE AND KNOWLEDGE OF STUDENTS BECOMES A POWERFUL ENGINE FOR OUR WORK. THEY BECOME AUTHORS, ARTISTS, INTELLECTUALS, SCIENTISTS, COMPOSERS, HEALERS, ARCHITECTS, INVENTORS, CREATORS, CITIZENS.

I WANT TO BUILD SPACES WHERE THE INSISTENTLY SOCIAL NATURE OF LEARNING IS HONORED, WHERE KNOWLEDGE AND POWER ARE SHARED AND NOT HOARDED. KNOWLEDGE, LIKE LOVE, IS SOMETHING YOU CAN GIVE AWAY WITHOUT LOSING A THING.

I WANT TO BUILD SPACES WHERE INTELLIGENCE — BROAD, OPEN, MULTIDIMENSIONAL — IS JUST ASSUMED, AND WHERE THE FLOW BETWEEN FAMILY, COMMUNITY, CULTURE, AND CLASSROOM IS SEAMLESS. THERE MUST BE A RANGE OF WAYS TO SUCCEED, MULTIPLE INTERESTS TO PURSUE, A VARIETY OF CONTRIBUTIONS TO MAKE.

I WANT TO BUILD SPACES WHERE THERE'S LOTS OF ROOM TO ASK QUESTIONS OF THE WORLD, TO INTERROGATE COMMON SENSE, TO CHALLENGE THE ORTHODOX. WHY? WHY? WHY? I WANT MY CLASSROOM TO BE UNSETTLED IN THIS WAY. I WANT STUDENTS TO HAVE A SENSE OF CURIOSITY AND WONDER AND ASTONISHMENT.

I WANT TO BUILD SPACES THAT NOURISH OUR IMAGINATION, SENSE THAT THE WORLD IS BIG AND DELICIOUS, AND FRAGILE AND PRECIOUS, DYNAMIC AND ALWAYS IN FLUX. ANOTHER WORLD IS POSSIBLE—AND INEVITABLE—AND WE CAN PARTICIPATE AND IMPACT THE FUTURE.

I WANT TO BUILD SPACES WHERE STUDENTS ARE NURTURED AND CHALLENGED IN THE SAME GESTURE, WHERE THEY HAVE FULL ACCESS TO ALL THE LITERACIES OF OUR TIME AND PLACE, AND WHERE THEY ALSO DEVELOP THE DISPOSITIONS OF MIND THAT WILL ALLOW THEM TO SHAPE AND RESHAPE THE WORLD.

I WANT TO BUILD SPACES WHERE LIFE IS LIVED IN THE PRESENT TENSE—WHERE LIFE IN SCHOOL IS LIFE ITSELF, KINDNESS BEGETS KINDNESS, ACCOMPLISHMENT REPEATS ITSELF. I TRY TO DEVELOP A PERMANENT READINESS FOR THE MARVELOUS.

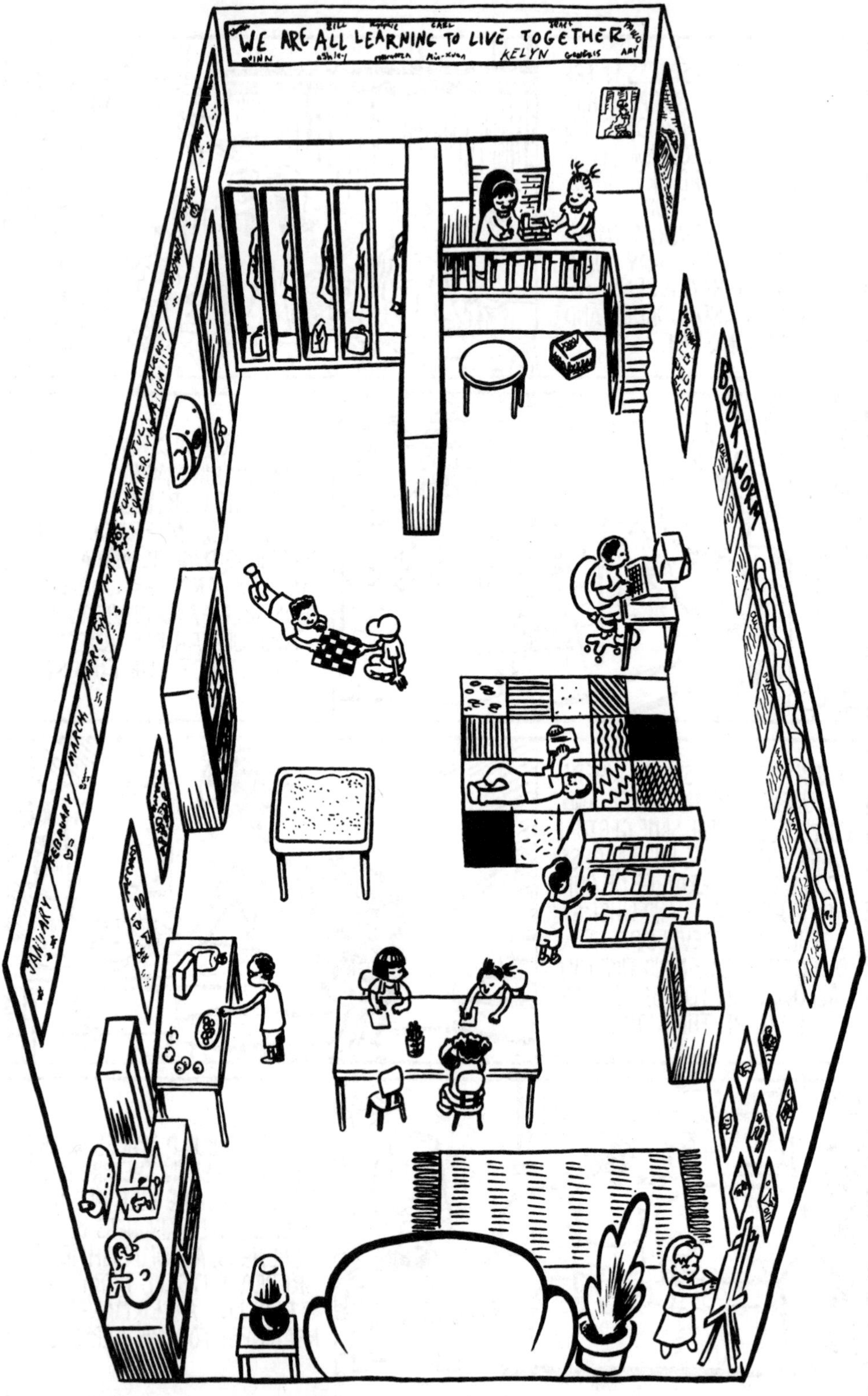
WE ARE ALL LEARNING TO LIVE TOGETHER
BILL
CARL
ashley
KELYN
ARY
JANUARY
FEBRUARY
MARCH
APRIL
MAY
JUNE
JULY
AUGUST
BOOK WORM

4

BUILDING BRIDGES

TEACHING IS OFTEN BRIDGE-BUILDING. BEGINNING ON ONE
SHORE WITH THE KNOWLEDGE, EXPERIENCE, KNOW-HOW,
AND INTERESTS OF THE STUDENT, THE TEACHER MOVES
TOWARD BROADER HORIZONS AND DEEPER WAYS OF
KNOWING.

BINGO'S NEVER IN A HURRY, HE JUST LUMP, LUMP, LUMP, LUMP!

HE'S SLOW.

HE'S FAST FOR HIM!

HE'S SLOW.

BUT HIS SHELL IS HEAVY.

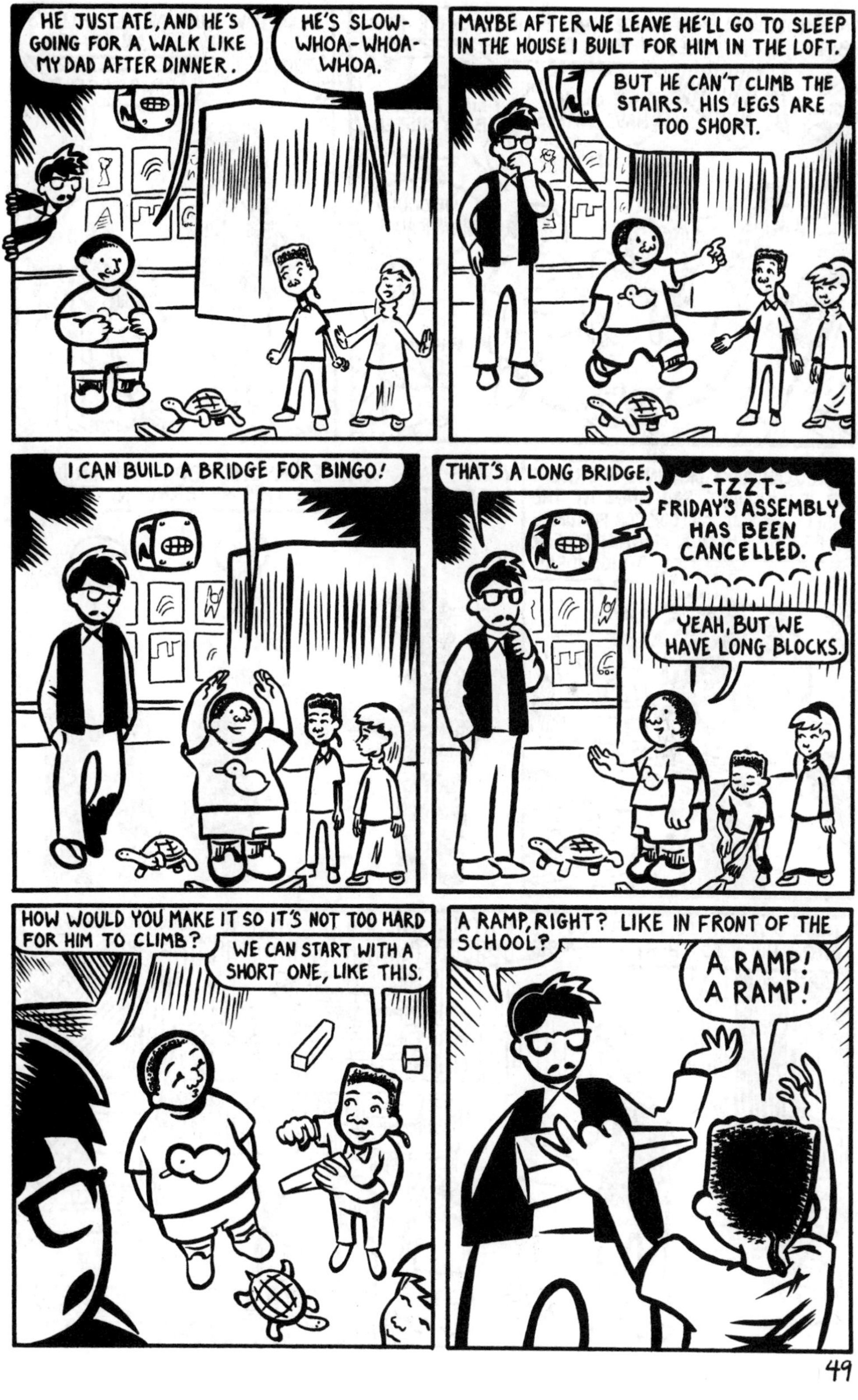
HE JUST ATE, AND HE'S GOING FOR A WALK LIKE MY DAD AFTER DINNER.
HE'S SLOW-WHOA-WHOA-WHOA.
MAYBE AFTER WE LEAVE HE'LL GO TO SLEEP IN THE HOUSE I BUILT FOR HIM IN THE LOFT.
BUT HE CAN'T CLIMB THE STAIRS. HIS LEGS ARE TOO SHORT.
I CAN BUILD A BRIDGE FOR BINGO!
THAT'S A LONG BRIDGE.
-TZZT- FRIDAY'S ASSEMBLY HAS BEEN CANCELLED.
YEAH, BUT WE HAVE LONG BLOCKS.
HOW WOULD YOU MAKE IT SO IT'S NOT TOO HARD FOR HIM TO CLIMB?
WE CAN START WITH A SHORT ONE, LIKE THIS.
A RAMP, RIGHT? LIKE IN FRONT OF THE SCHOOL?
A RAMP! A RAMP!

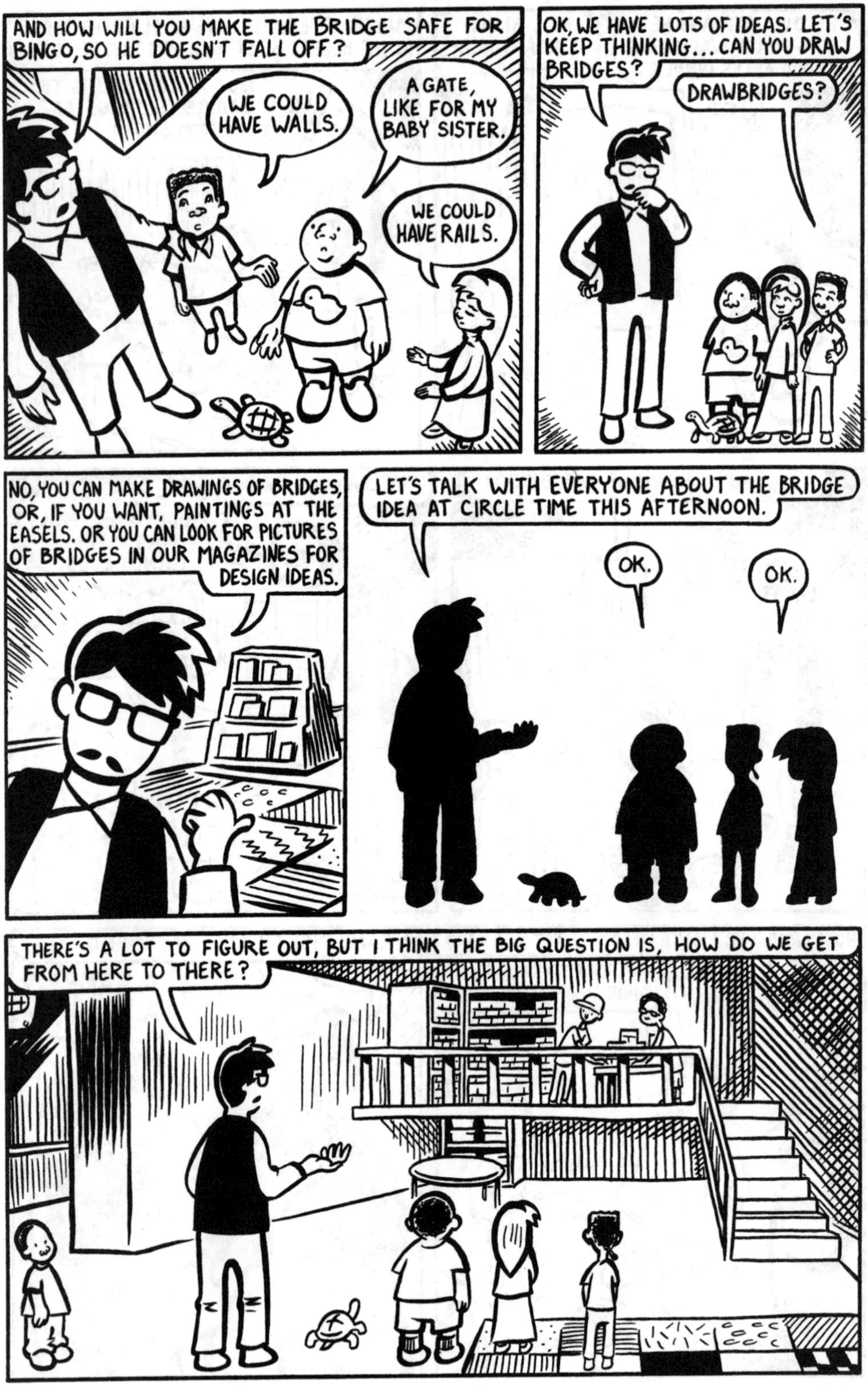
AND HOW WILL YOU MAKE THE BRIDGE SAFE FOR BINGO, SO HE DOESN'T FALL OFF?
WE COULD HAVE WALLS.
A GATE, LIKE FOR MY BABY SISTER.
WE COULD HAVE RAILS.
OK, WE HAVE LOTS OF IDEAS. LET'S KEEP THINKING... CAN YOU DRAW BRIDGES?
DRAWBRIDGES?
NO, YOU CAN MAKE DRAWINGS OF BRIDGES, OR, IF YOU WANT, PAINTINGS AT THE EASELS. OR YOU CAN LOOK FOR PICTURES OF BRIDGES IN OUR MAGAZINES FOR DESIGN IDEAS.
LET'S TALK WITH EVERYONE ABOUT THE BRIDGE IDEA AT CIRCLE TIME THIS AFTERNOON.
OK.
OK.
THERE'S A LOT TO FIGURE OUT, BUT I THINK THE BIG QUESTION IS, HOW DO WE GET FROM HERE TO THERE?

WHEN OUR OLDEST SON, ZAYD, WAS 12, HE ATTENDED A FRIEND'S BAR MITZVAH.

ALL THE RITUALS FASCINATED HIM — THE ANCIENT TEXTS AND SYMBOLS, THE SPEECHES AND PERFORMANCES, THE SPIRITUAL INVOCATION, THE CHARGE OF NEW RESPONSIBILITY ACCOMPANYING NEW FREEDOMS.

בָּרוּךְ אַתָּה יְיָ, אֱלֹהֵינוּ מֶלֶךְ הָעוֹלָם, אֲשֶׁר נָתַן לָנוּ תּוֹרַת אֱמֶת וְחַיֵּי עוֹלָם נָטַע בְּתוֹכֵנוּ. בָּרוּךְ אַתָּה יְיָ, נוֹתֵן הַתּוֹרָה.

HE WAS GROWING AND STRETCHING THROUGHOUT THE CEREMONY, AND IN THE END HE EVEN _LOOKED_ DIFFERENT.

ZAYD WANTED TO ORGANIZE A CEREMONY FOR HIMSELF, SOME KIND OF RITUAL TO MARK HIS OWN BRIDGE FROM CHILDHOOD TO ADULTHOOD. HIS MOM, BERNARDINE, BECAME MENTOR, GUIDE, AND FELLOW TRAVELER.

THEY BEGAN THEIR JOURNEY BY RAISING QUESTIONS AT THE FAMILY TABLE. WHAT DOES IT MEAN TO BECOME AN ADULT? WHICH CHANGES ARE MEASURABLE AND WHICH ARE ABOUT QUALITY AND CHARACTER? DO ADULTS THINK DIFFERENTLY THAN KIDS? HOW MUCH OF WHO WE ARE IS DETERMINED GENETICALLY OR BIOLOGICALLY, AND HOW MUCH SOCIALLY OR CULTURALLY?

ZAYD'S EXPLORATION WAS ENHANCED BY A SERIES OF READINGS THAT HE AND BERNARDINE SELECTED: TRADITIONAL NOVELS LIKE *LITTLE WOMEN* AND *DAVID COPPERFIELD*, AUTOBIOGRAPHIES LIKE *MALCOLM X*, *ANNE FRANK*, AND *COMING OF AGE IN MISSISSIPPI*, STORIES LIKE *THE EDUCATION OF LITTLE TREE* AND *THE RED BADGE OF COURAGE*. ZAYD'S GREATEST INSPIRATION CAME FROM MARI SANDOZ'S STORY OF *CRAZY HORSE*, THE SIOUX LEADER KNOWN AS THE "STRANGE MAN OF THE OGLALAS."

ZAYD BUILT A CEREMONY INSPIRED BY NATIVE AMERICAN LORE. HE STARTED BY CREATING "THE SYMBOLS OF MY LIFE," PRIMITIVE-LOOKING MARKINGS THAT SIGNIFIED CONCEPTION,   GROWTH,   CHILDHOOD,   ADULTHOOD,   AND DEATH.

HE CHALLENGED HIMSELF TO CREATE A SET OF CRAFTS THAT WOULD NEATLY INCORPORATE THESE SYMBOLS.

BECAUSE HE WAS THE ARCHITECT AND OWNER OF THE CEREMONY, THE WORK INSPIRED SUSTAINED EFFORT AND STEADY COMMITMENT.

HE SETTLED ON 3 CRAFTS, AND WROTE A PASSAGE ABOUT EACH:

A CEREMONIAL BUCKSKIN SHIELD

I'm going to make it simple but beautiful, because too much detail crowds the essence of things.

A BUCKSKIN VEST

I will wear this on my vision quest. In this, like the shield, I am trying to achieve beautiful simplicity.

A COUP STICK

This will not be a weapon used for killing, but instead my medicine, symbolizing my personal struggles and victories.

ZAYD DECIDED HE DIDN'T WANT A PARTY OF ANY KIND, BUT WANTED INSTEAD TO TAKE HIS CRAFTS TO A QUIET PLACE ALONE TO FAST AND SEEK A VISION, JUST LIKE CRAZY HORSE HAD DONE ON HIS BIRTHDAY. HE TREKKED OUT TO A STRETCH OF DUNES ON THE BEACH WHILE WE WAITED...

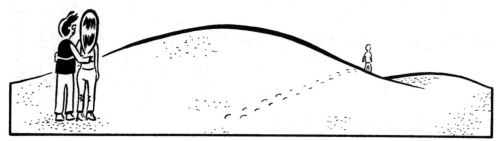

First there was an empty ocean beach, and then came a fire and out of this fire stepped a man.

Onto this beach came a buffalo.

The man took his bow and shot the buffalo. The arrow would have missed, but the buffalo turned so that it hit him. The man ate the meat and suddenly knew all the things that animals know as well as all things that men know.

The man then went back to his people and walked through the streets and the people saw him and most of them walked with him because they all wanted to get where he was going.

Some people did not walk with him because they were scared. So they never got there and there were some people who ran ahead, but they got tired too quickly and didn't get there.

At last, the people got to the beach where the man had killed the buffalo.

54

The man started singing to them and all the knowledge of the animals flowed out of him like a rainbow and into the people so that they knew all these things.

But the man was still sad he had killed the buffalo, so he held up a shining piece of metal and all the people started singing with him. The rainbow flowed out of them and into the metal and all of a sudden, the buffalo was there.

The man was happy, but he'd used up too much of himself bringing back the buffalo, so he walked into the sea and lay down on the ocean floor.

As he lay there, he aged very quickly, but instead of growing weaker he grew wiser. As he was about to die, he saw that his people were about to kill the buffalo and reclaim the knowledge of animals.

With his last dying breath he sang again and the knowledge poured from his lips and into the people and they saw they should not kill the buffalo.

Seeing this, the man knew he had fulfilled his purpose, and finally died.

WHEN ZAYD RETURNED, HE WAS INDEED TRANSFORMED, HIS COMING OF AGE COMPLETE.

THE PATH TO ADULTHOOD ISN'T ALL SWEETNESS AND LIGHT, BUT ZAYD SHOWED US A GENEROUS AND UPLIFTING AFFIRMATION OF ADOLESCENCE. "I WAS A TEENAGE WEREWOLF" IS AN ENDURING POPULAR METAPHOR, BUT ZAYD HAD FLIPPED THE SCRIPT AND REFUSED A PART IN SOMEONE ELSE'S B-MOVIE PLOT.

THE BRIDGE FROM CHILDHOOD IS LONG AND COMPLEX, BUILT BLOCK BY BLOCK.

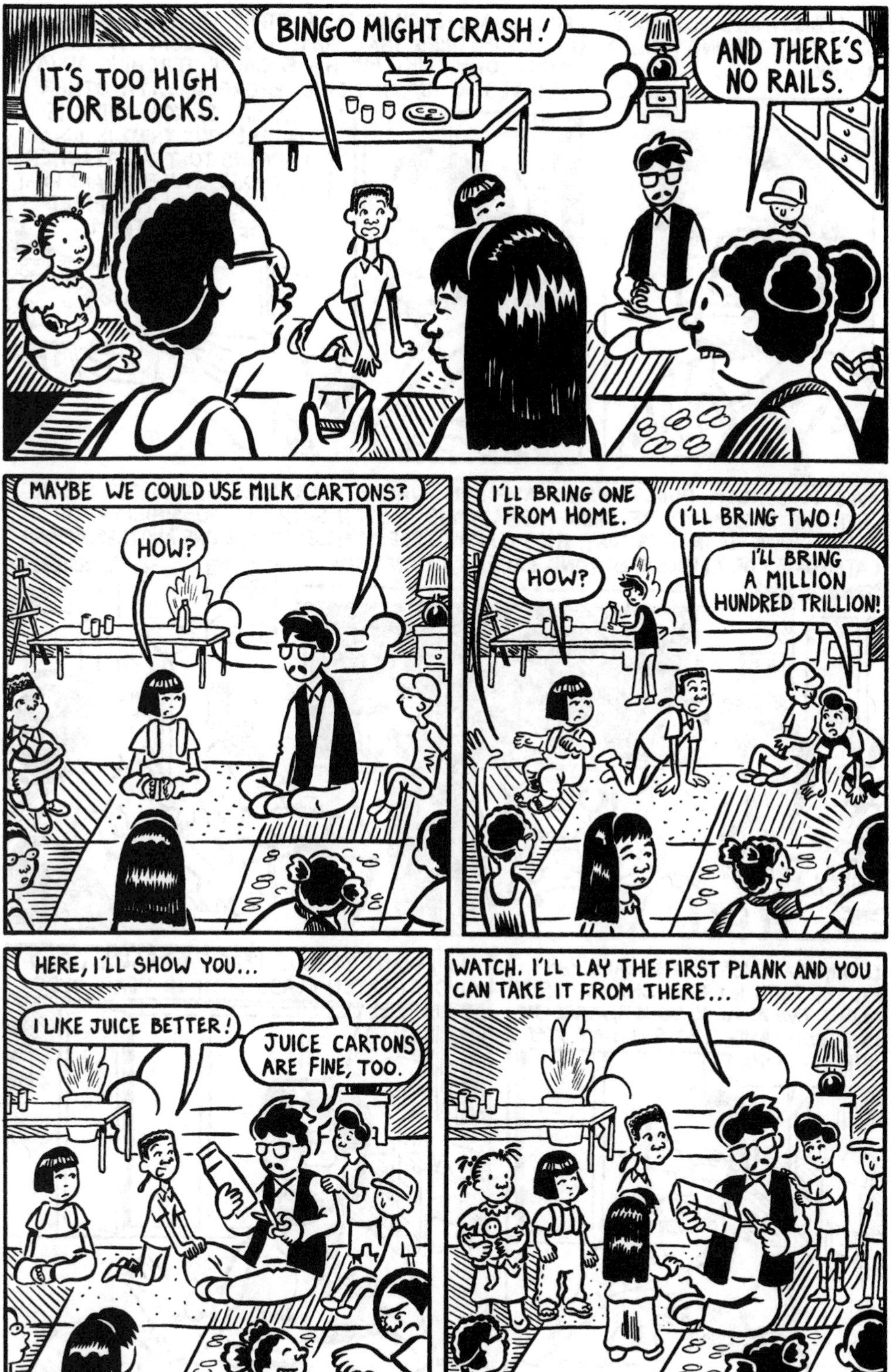
IT'S TOO HIGH FOR BLOCKS.
BINGO MIGHT CRASH!
AND THERE'S NO RAILS.
MAYBE WE COULD USE MILK CARTONS?
HOW?
I'LL BRING ONE FROM HOME.
HOW?
I'LL BRING TWO!
I'LL BRING A MILLION HUNDRED TRILLION!
HERE, I'LL SHOW YOU...
I LIKE JUICE BETTER!
JUICE CARTONS ARE FINE, TOO.
WATCH. I'LL LAY THE FIRST PLANK AND YOU CAN TAKE IT FROM THERE...

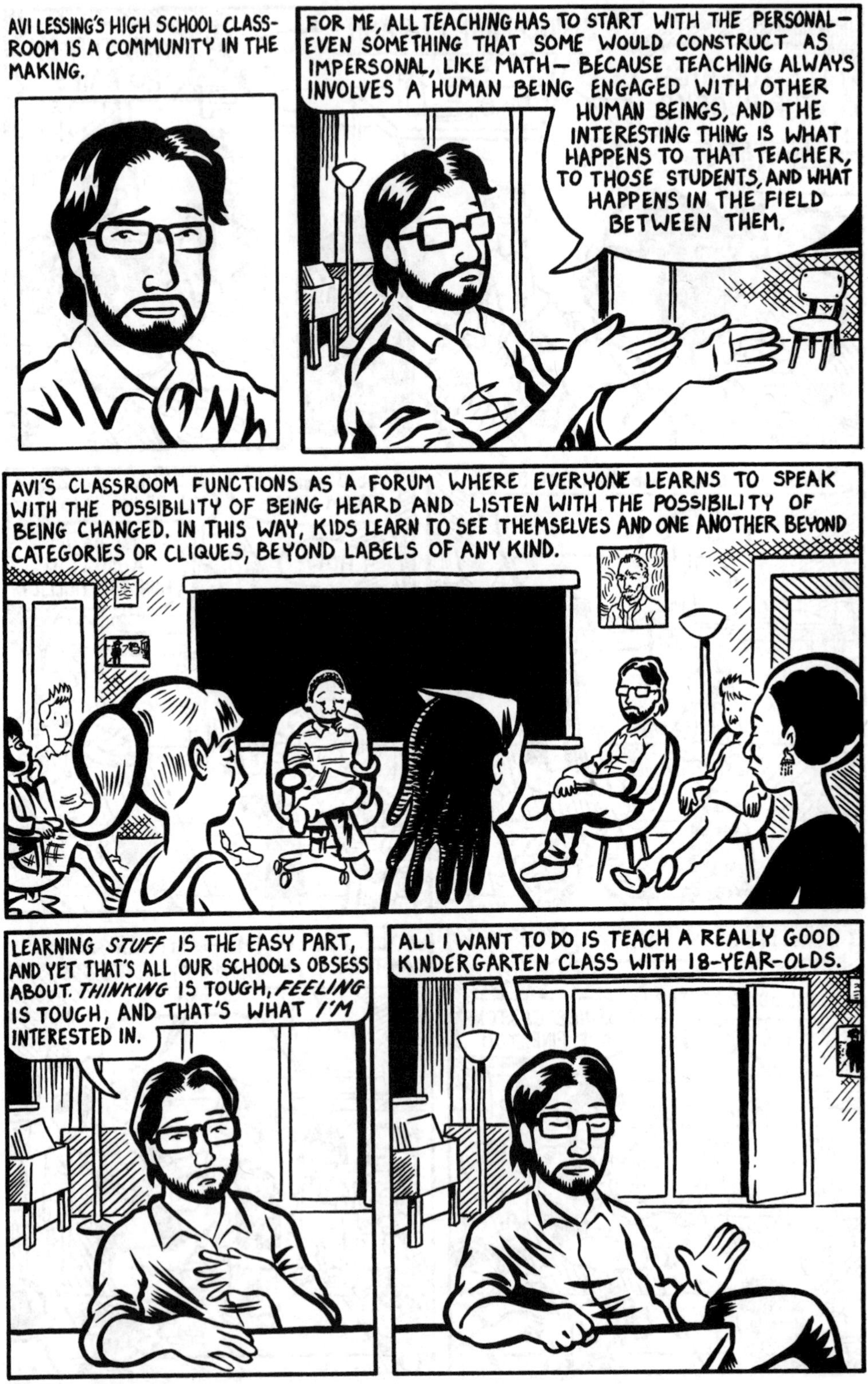
AVI LESSING'S HIGH SCHOOL CLASSROOM IS A COMMUNITY IN THE MAKING.
FOR ME, ALL TEACHING HAS TO START WITH THE PERSONAL— EVEN SOMETHING THAT SOME WOULD CONSTRUCT AS IMPERSONAL, LIKE MATH— BECAUSE TEACHING ALWAYS INVOLVES A HUMAN BEING ENGAGED WITH OTHER HUMAN BEINGS, AND THE INTERESTING THING IS WHAT HAPPENS TO THAT TEACHER, TO THOSE STUDENTS, AND WHAT HAPPENS IN THE FIELD BETWEEN THEM.
AVI'S CLASSROOM FUNCTIONS AS A FORUM WHERE EVERYONE LEARNS TO SPEAK WITH THE POSSIBILITY OF BEING HEARD AND LISTEN WITH THE POSSIBILITY OF BEING CHANGED. IN THIS WAY, KIDS LEARN TO SEE THEMSELVES AND ONE ANOTHER BEYOND CATEGORIES OR CLIQUES, BEYOND LABELS OF ANY KIND.
LEARNING *STUFF* IS THE EASY PART, AND YET THAT'S ALL OUR SCHOOLS OBSESS ABOUT. *THINKING* IS TOUGH, *FEELING* IS TOUGH, AND THAT'S WHAT *I'M* INTERESTED IN.
ALL I WANT TO DO IS TEACH A REALLY GOOD KINDERGARTEN CLASS WITH 18-YEAR-OLDS.

RACE, GENDER, LOVE, DEATH, DRUGS, SEXUALITY, PLEASURE, PAIN, DISEASE— THESE ARE ALL REGULAR TOPICS OF DISCUSSION IN AVI'S WORLD.

ONE DAY A WHITE STUDENT WAS PRESENTING A STORY IN CLASS ABOUT ICE SKATING AND VEERED INTO UNWELCOME TERRITORY...

THERE'S, LIKE, NEVER ANY BLACK KIDS AT THE SKATING RINK. OMG, WHAT'S THAT THING CHRIS ROCK SAYS? "MY MOMMA COULDN'T BUY NO ICE SKATES..." OR WAS THAT DAVE CHAPELLE?

OH YEAH, TOTALLY! "BRUTHAS ON ICE" OR SOMETHING...

EXCUSE ME...

DUDE, THAT WAS EDDIE MURPHY...

EXCUSE ME, THIS IS A RACIST CONVERSATION.

WHAT? I DIDN'T MEAN...

UH-UH. YOU'RE IN HERE TALKING ABOUT "BLACK PEOPLE CAN'T AFFORD ICE SKATES" LIKE IT'S FUNNY. THERE ARE RACIST PEOPLE IN HERE.

:SOB: THAT'S *NOT* WHAT I MEANT!

MISTY, WAIT...

YOU SEE? THAT'S JUST WHAT I MEAN — *SHE* MAKES A RACIST COMMENT, AND NO ONE RUNS OVER TO COMFORT *ME*. NOW *SHE'S* GOT TO BE TAKEN CARE OF, AND HERE *I* AM.

AVI LET THIS ALL UNFOLD, AND HE QUESTIONED HIMSELF. ARE THESE CONVERSATIONS USEFUL? IS IT APPROPRIATE TO OPEN ALL THESE DOORS? ARE THERE SOME THINGS BETTER LEFT UNSAID OR UNEXPLORED?

WHITE PRIVILEGE IS A HIDDEN CURRICULUM THROUGHOUT OUR SOCIETY— RACIAL HIERARCHIES, THE INEVITABLE MISUNDERSTANDINGS, ASPIRATIONS, TRIALS, AND ERRORS BECOME POINTS OF INVESTIGATION IN AVI'S WORLD. NO NEAT CONCLUSIONS ARE REACHED, ONLY THE RISKY ROAD OF HONESTY AND RESPONSIBILITY, THE NECESSARY PASSAGE TO COMMUNITY.

THE DISCUSSION THAT FOLLOWED MOVED EVERYONE, BUT SETTLED NOTHING. RACISM DIDN'T END THAT DAY DESPITE AVI'S BEST EFFORTS TO FACILITATE A CONSTRUCTIVE DIALOGUE. HE FELT THAT THE BRIDGE HE WAS TRYING TO BUILD REMAINED UNFINISHED. THAT EVENING HE CALLED HIS MOTHER, A THERAPIST, QUESTIONING WHETHER HIS TEACHING HAD ANY VALUE WHATSOEVER.

YOU BELONG THERE BECAUSE YOU'RE STILL ABLE TO ASK THAT QUESTION.

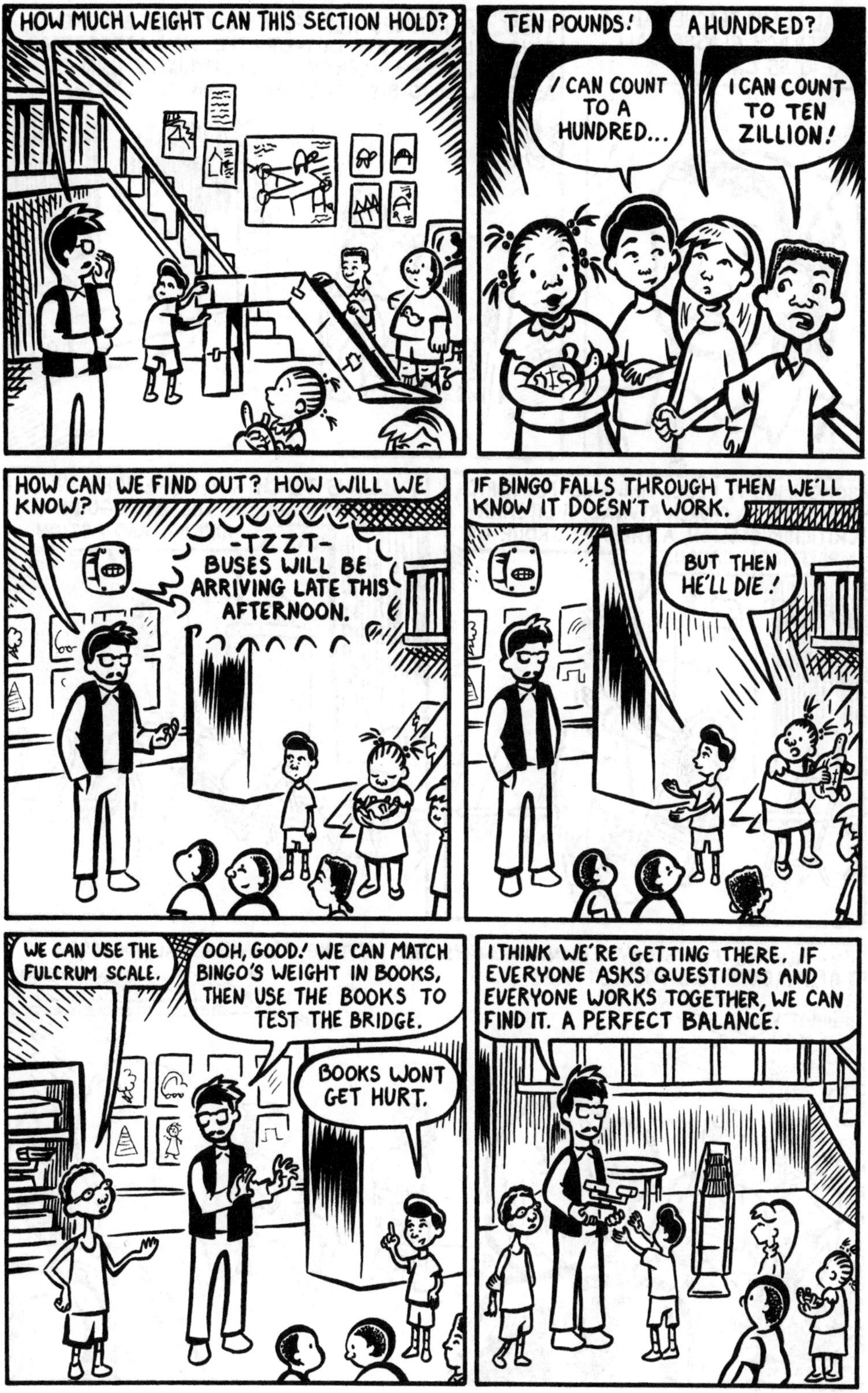
HOW MUCH WEIGHT CAN THIS SECTION HOLD?
TEN POUNDS!
A HUNDRED?
I CAN COUNT TO A HUNDRED...
I CAN COUNT TO TEN ZILLION!
HOW CAN WE FIND OUT? HOW WILL WE KNOW?
-TZZT- BUSES WILL BE ARRIVING LATE THIS AFTERNOON.
IF BINGO FALLS THROUGH THEN WE'LL KNOW IT DOESN'T WORK.
BUT THEN HE'LL DIE!
WE CAN USE THE FULCRUM SCALE.
OOH, GOOD! WE CAN MATCH BINGO'S WEIGHT IN BOOKS, THEN USE THE BOOKS TO TEST THE BRIDGE.
BOOKS WONT GET HURT.
I THINK WE'RE GETTING THERE. IF EVERYONE ASKS QUESTIONS AND EVERYONE WORKS TOGETHER, WE CAN FIND IT. A PERFECT BALANCE.

SAL ADAMS TEACHES ADULT LITERACY CLASSES ALL ACROSS CHICAGO.

THESE GATHERINGS TAKE PLACE IN CHURCH BASEMENTS, SCHOOL LUNCHROOMS, OUT-OF-THE-WAY CAFETERIAS, DONUT SHOPS— WHEREVER A COMMUNITY CAN BE ASSEMBLED TO SIT TOGETHER, THINK, AND WRITE.

SOMETIMES IT FEELS LIKE A COFFEE KLATCH, OTHER TIMES A CHURCH REVIVAL, A LITERARY CRITICISM SESSION, A THERAPY GROUP, OR A POLITICAL CAUCUS...

I ALWAYS TEACH WITH ONE IDEA IN MIND: EXPERIENCE IS THE BEST GUIDE TO THINKING AND ACTION.

BUT ALWAYS THE STORYTELLING, ALWAYS THE WRITING, ALWAYS A KALEIDESCOPE OF ENACTMENTS AND POSSIBILITIES.

SAL WORKS IN POOR COMMUNITIES AND TRIES TO CREATE OPPORTUNITIES FOR PEOPLE TO BECOME MORE INTENTIONAL AND MORE CAPABLE IN THEIR OWN PROJECTS AND PURSUITS.

HER STUDENTS STRUGGLE TO READ THE WORD AS THEY "READ" THE WORLD.

IN ONE CLASS THE WRITING WAS PROMPTED BY A SIMPLE STORY-STARTER:

WHAT DID YOU SEE ON YOUR WAY HERE THIS MORNING?

GLORIA WROTE ABOUT AN ABANDONED BUILDING ON THE BLOCK, NOW A DRUG HOUSE.

THE PLACE SCARED HER AND HER KIDS, AND AS SHE READ, SEVERAL WOMEN IN THE CIRCLE SAID, "AMEN," AND AGREED THAT THE PLACE WAS A MENACE. WHAT HAD BEEN EXPERIENCED AS PRIVATE BECAME SOCIAL AND SHARED.

FOR THE NEXT SEVERAL WEEKS, THE HOUSE BECAME A FOCUS OF WRITING AND CONVERSATION.

WHEN SAL SUGGESTED THEY INVESTIGATE HOW TO GET THE CITY TO RETRIEVE THE LOT, THE GROUP SPRANG INTO ACTION.

WITHIN A YEAR THE LOT HAD BEEN RECLAIMED AND THE WOMEN HAD OFFICIALLY FOUNDED THE "WEST-TOWN THINKING TANK," IN ORDER, AS THEY SAID, "TO STUDY PROBLEMS IN OUR COMMUNITY AND THEN ACT TO CHANGE THEM AROUND."

THE GROUP PRODUCED A PUBLICATION, CALLED *THE JOURNAL OF ORDINARY THOUGHT,* TO BE CIRCULATED IN THE COMMUNITY FOR COMMENT AND DISCUSSION.

EACH EDITION HAD A STATEMENT OF PURPOSE POSTED FRONT AND CENTER:

THE JOURNAL OF ORDINARY THOUGHT

THE JOURNAL PUBLISHES REFLECTIONS ON THE PROPOSITION THAT EVERY PERSON IS A PHILOSOPHER, EXPRESSING ONE'S THOUGHTS FOSTERS CREATIVITY AND CHANGE, AND TAKING CONTROL OF LIFE REQUIRES PEOPLE TO THINK ABOUT THE WORLD AND COMMUNICATE THEIR THOUGHTS TO OTHERS.

SAL BELIEVES THAT ORDINARY PEOPLE HOLD THE KEY TO A BETTER FUTURE. THROUGH A TEACHING COMMUNITY, THEY LEARN TO THINK FOR THEMSELVES AND ACHIEVE THEIR GOALS. THEY HAVE THE RIGHT TO THINK AND ACT RATHER THAN RELY ON SOME AUTHORITY OR LEADER TO DO IT FOR THEM.

EACH PERSON IS AN EXPERT ON HIS OR HER OWN EXPERIENCE... THE PEOPLE WITH THE PROBLEMS ARE ALSO THE PEOPLE WITH THE SOLUTIONS. TEACHING HERE IS NOT HIERARCHICAL OR PATRONIZING, BUT HORIZONTAL AND SHARED.

SAL IS HERSELF A BRIDGE FROM THE MARGIN TOWARD THE CENTER, FROM THE POWERLESS TO POWER.

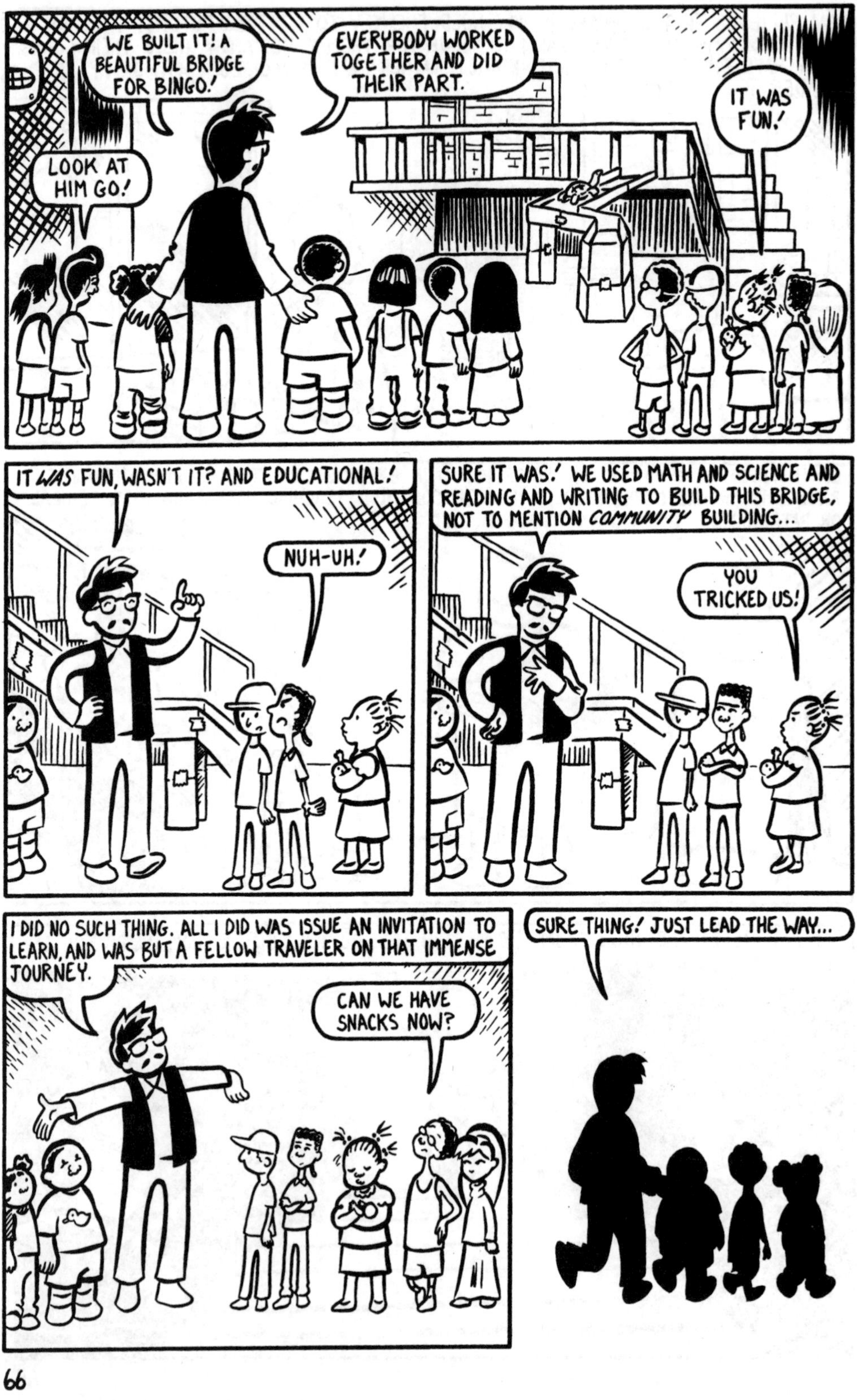
WE BUILT IT! A BEAUTIFUL BRIDGE FOR BINGO!
EVERYBODY WORKED TOGETHER AND DID THEIR PART.
LOOK AT HIM GO!
IT WAS FUN!
IT WAS FUN, WASN'T IT? AND EDUCATIONAL!
NUH-UH!
SURE IT WAS! WE USED MATH AND SCIENCE AND READING AND WRITING TO BUILD THIS BRIDGE, NOT TO MENTION COMMUNITY BUILDING...
YOU TRICKED US!
I DID NO SUCH THING. ALL I DID WAS ISSUE AN INVITATION TO LEARN, AND WAS BUT A FELLOW TRAVELER ON THAT IMMENSE JOURNEY.
CAN WE HAVE SNACKS NOW?
SURE THING! JUST LEAD THE WAY...

5
LIBERATING THE CURRICULUM

CURRICULUM IS MORE THAN PIECES OF INFORMATION, MORE
THAN SUBJECT MATTER, MORE EVEN THAN THE DISCIPLINES.
CURRICULUM IS AN ONGOING ENGAGEMENT WITH THE
PROBLEM OF DETERMINING WHAT KNOWLEDGE AND
EXPERIENCES ARE MOST WORTHWHILE. WITH EACH PERSON
AND EACH SITUATION, THAT PROBLEM TAKES ON UNIQUE
SHADINGS AND DIFFERENT MEANINGS.

as Chief Executive. He brought to the Presidency the rigid dispositions of mind of his Scottish heritage as well as a sense of destiny and the pious teachings of his father and his father-in-law, both Presbyterian ministers.

In equal measure he brought dazzling intellectual gifts and credentials: educated at Princeton, he graduated from the University of Virginia Law School and went on to earn a Doctorate in Government from Johns Hopkins University. He taught at Wesleyan and Bryn Mawr before returning to Princeton as professor of political economy and jurisprudence, where he later served as president for eight years, starting in 1902.

Woodrow Wilson's big brain was matched by his pragmatic heart, and he found himself often chomping at the bit, eager to try out his reformist ideas in the real rough and tumble world of practical life. In 1911 he dived head-first from the ivory tower into the political mix, becoming Governor of New Jersey. And in 1912, when Teddy Roosevelt and William Howard Taft split the Republican vote, Wilson became President.

Difficulties Facing the President

In his first term, Wilson supported and passed America's first-ever federal progressive income tax.

Woodrow Wilson-The People's Choice, the Last Straw

In a move that led to noisy protests from civil rights groups, and is still criticized today, Wilson supported segregation in many federally funded agencies, and this support led to widespread firing of black workers.

Wilson's second term centered on WWI. He had based his re-election campaign on the slogan, "He kept us out of war!" but US neutrality was short-lived. When the German Foreign Secretary offered to return Arizona, New Mexico and Texas to Mexico if they would ally with Germany in the event of war, Wilson asked Congress to declare war in April 1917.

In the late stages of war, Wilson issued his famous fourteen points, his view of a post-war world that

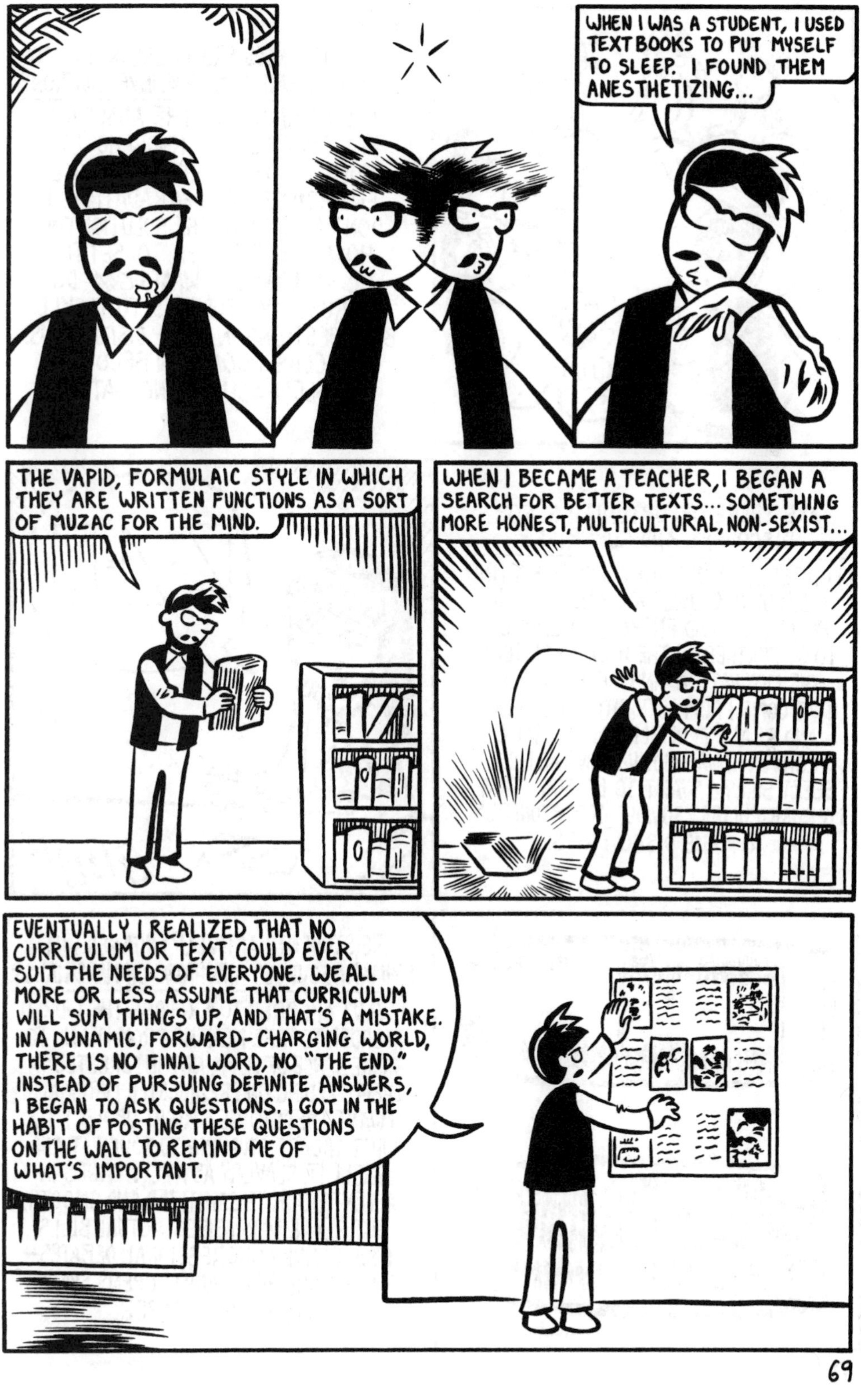
WHEN I WAS A STUDENT, I USED TEXTBOOKS TO PUT MYSELF TO SLEEP. I FOUND THEM ANESTHETIZING...
THE VAPID, FORMULAIC STYLE IN WHICH THEY ARE WRITTEN FUNCTIONS AS A SORT OF MUZAC FOR THE MIND.
WHEN I BECAME A TEACHER, I BEGAN A SEARCH FOR BETTER TEXTS... SOMETHING MORE HONEST, MULTICULTURAL, NON-SEXIST...
EVENTUALLY I REALIZED THAT NO CURRICULUM OR TEXT COULD EVER SUIT THE NEEDS OF EVERYONE. WE ALL MORE OR LESS ASSUME THAT CURRICULUM WILL SUM THINGS UP, AND THAT'S A MISTAKE. IN A DYNAMIC, FORWARD-CHARGING WORLD, THERE IS NO FINAL WORD, NO "THE END." INSTEAD OF PURSUING DEFINITE ANSWERS, I BEGAN TO ASK QUESTIONS. I GOT IN THE HABIT OF POSTING THESE QUESTIONS ON THE WALL TO REMIND ME OF WHAT'S IMPORTANT.

ARE CHALLENGES FROM CLASSROOM TO COMMUNITY FAIR GAME FOR INVESTIGATION?

I DON'T KNOW ALL THE ANSWERS. NOT ONLY DO I NOT KNOW HOW TO SOLVE GLOBAL PROBLEMS LIKE ENVIRONMENTAL DEGRADATION, I DON'T EVEN KNOW THE SOLUTION FOR HOW TO GET KELYN TO SETTLE DOWN AND FOCUS. WHAT I *CAN* DO IS TRUST MY STUDENTS TO TACKLE BIG QUESTIONS IN GROUP DISCUSSIONS. OUR CLASSROOM CAN BECOME A PROBLEM-SOLVING INCUBATOR.

ARE THERE OPPORTUNITIES FOR DISCOVERY AND SURPRISE?

I'M INTERESTED IN STUDENTS CONSTRUCTING THEIR OWN KNOWLEDGE AND FEELING POWERFUL AND ENERGIZED ENOUGH TO GO FURTHER IN THEIR EXPECTATIONS. THE MOTIVATION AND SELF-ESTEEM THAT COME FROM AUTHENTIC DISCOVERY AND REAL ACCOMPLISHMENT MAKE CONVENTIONAL MOTIVATION TACTICS SEEM SILLY. I WANT TO BE SURE THAT MY CURRICULUM PROVIDES OPPORTUNITIES TO MAKE DISCOVERIES.

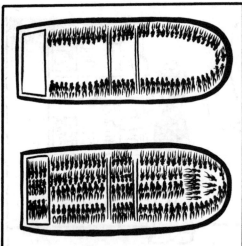

ARE STUDENTS ACTIVELY ENGAGED WITH PRIMARY SOURCES AND HANDS-ON MATERIALS?

I WANT CHILDREN TO EXPLORE THE WORLD IN ORDER TO TAKE MEANING FROM IT AND TO MAKE SENSE OF IT. I'M NOT INTERESTED IN THEIR FEEDING ON PREDIGESTED MATERIALS; I WANT THEM TO GET RIGHT UP NEXT TO WHAT THEY'RE STUDYING, TO TOUCH IT AND SMELL IT. SLAVERY AS A FEW PAGES IN A TEXTBOOK IS SANITIZED AND SMOOTH, BUT SLAVE NARRATIVES, ACTUAL BILLS OF SALE, AND CONGRESSIONAL DEBATES— THAT'S MORE REAL, AND IT OPENS SPACES FOR DIGGING DEEPER.

IS PRODUCTIVE WORK GOING ON?

I'M INTERESTED IN WORK THAT IS PURPOSEFUL AND ENGAGING FOR ME AND MY STUDENTS. I'M INTERESTED IN THE DIGNITY OF WORK, AND IN THE HUMAN DESIRE TO MARK OUR EXISTENCE THROUGH WORK. MUCH OF THE "WORK" OF SCHOOL IS NOT WORK AT ALL— IT IS MAKE-WORK OR BUSY-WORK, MEANINGLESS STUFF TO OCCUPY OUR TIME.

I WANT CLASSROOM WORK TO BE IMPORTANT TO STUDENTS, TO ME, AND WHEN POSSIBLE, TO THE LARGER COMMUNITY.

IS THE WORK LINKED TO STUDENT QUESTIONS OR INTERESTS?

I'M CONCERNED THAT SCHOOL BE A WELCOMING PLACE, A CREATIVE PLACE FOR STUDENTS TO WORK ON THEIR OWN CONCERNS. A LOT OF WHAT GOES ON IN SCHOOL IS OF THE "TAKE-THIS-PILL-BECAUSE-I-KNOW-WHAT'S-GOOD-FOR-YOU" VARIETY. I DON'T WANT MY CLASS TO DRIVE CHILDREN OUT; RATHER, I WANT TO DEVELOP MY AGENDA IN LIGHT OF THEIRS.

IS WORK IN MY CLASSROOM PURSUED TO ITS FAR LIMITS?

I OFTEN WONDER IF WE COULDN'T GO ONE MORE STEP, ASK ONE MORE QUESTION, BRING IN ONE MORE RESOURCE PERSON, TAKE ONE MORE TRIP, FIGURE OUT ONE MORE ACTIVITY. I WORRY THAT TOO MUCH OF WHAT KIDS EXPERIENCE IN SCHOOL IS SKIMMING ALONG THE SURFACE OF KNOWLEDGE AND NEVER REALLY PLUNGING IN. SOME TEACHERS SAY, "MAKE IT SIMPLE," BUT MY JOB IS KEEPING IT COMPLEX. COVERING A ZILLION ITEMS MAY NOT BE AS REWARDING AS PURSUING SOMETHING FULLY, DEEPLY, TRULY, AND WELL.

71

GOOD AFTERNOON, MR. AYERS. WE'RE HERE TODAY TO DISCUSS CURRICULUM STANDARDS.

COOL BEANS.

WE ADMIRE YOUR INGENUITY, BUT WE'RE CONCERNED THAT YOU TEACH EACH STUDENT TO MEET STATE REQUIREMENTS.

–TZZT– IS EVERYTHING QUIET?

RIGHT. "THE FULL DEVELOPMENT OF EACH IS THE NECESSARY CONDITION FOR THE FULL DEVELOPMENT OF ALL."

UM...SO WHAT ARE THE STANDARDS?

I'M GLAD YOU ASKED! WE'VE PROVIDED A CONVENIENT OUTLINE OF STATE GUIDELINES FOR YOU TO FOLLOW...

THESE WILL HELP YOU GAUGE STUDENT PROGRESS WITH CONFIDENCE AND PRECISION, AND PROVIDE THE NEEDED FOUNDATION FOR THEIR EDUCATIONAL CAREERS.

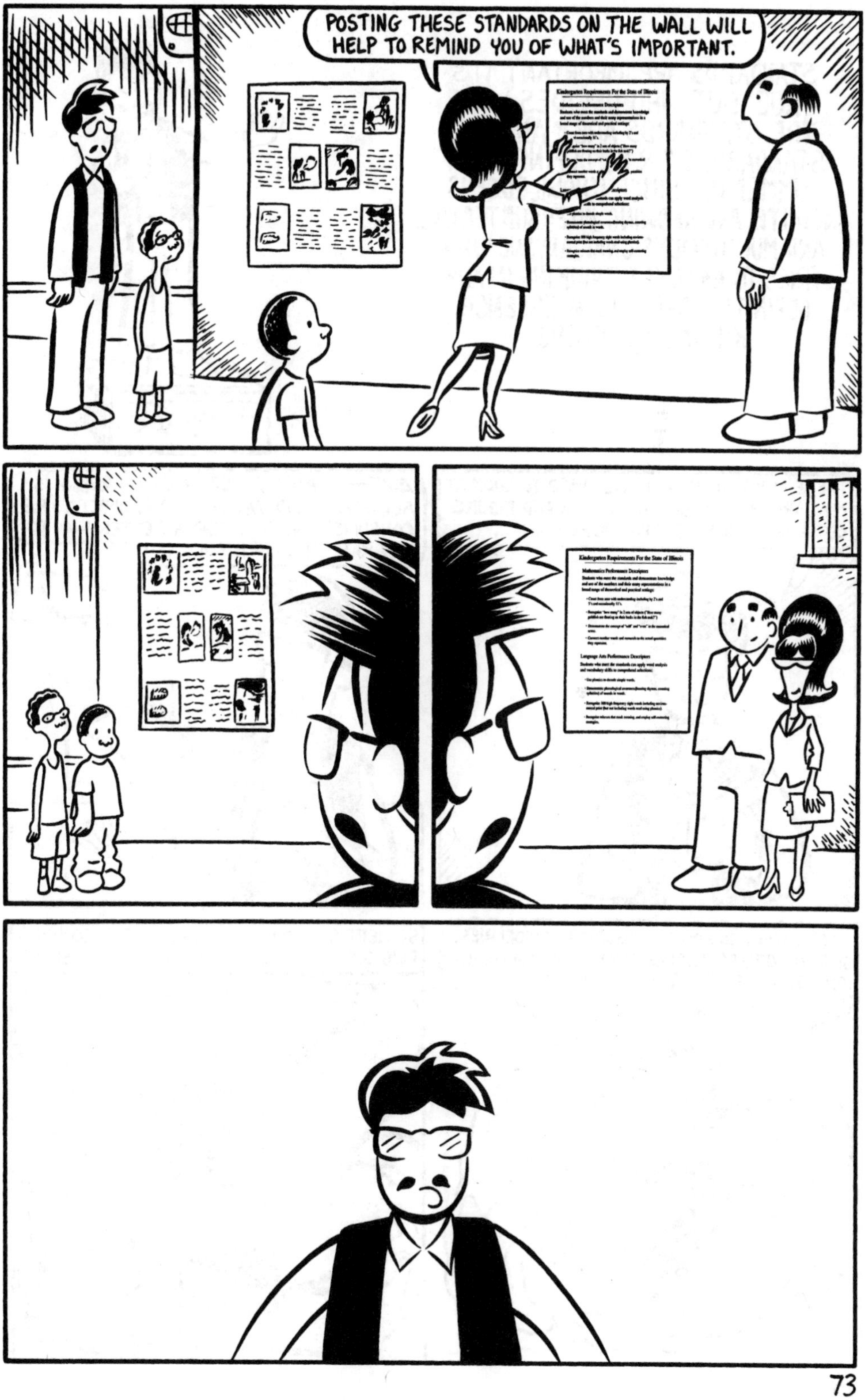
POSTING THESE STANDARDS ON THE WALL WILL HELP TO REMIND YOU OF WHAT'S IMPORTANT.
Kindergarten Requirements For the State of Illinois
Mathematics Performance Descriptors
Language Arts Performance Descriptors

STANDARDS ARE IMPORTANT, IT'S TRUE. BUT WHO DECIDES WHAT THE STANDARDS ARE? AND CAN STANDARDS EVER BE DEFINITIVELY SUMMED UP? SINCE KNOWLEDGE IS INFINITE, AND KNOWING INTERSUBJECTIVE AND MULTIDIMENSIONAL, ANYONE WHO TRIES TO BRACKET THINKING IN ANY DEFINITIVE SENSE IS, IN ESSENCE, KILLING LEARNING.

THERE MUST BE MORE. I STILL NEED TO LOOK AT MY LARGER PURPOSES AND GOALS AND FIGURE OUT HOW TO ASSESS HOW WE'RE DOING...

BUT— I CAN'T ACCEPT THAT LEARNING IS ALL *STUFF* AND *THINGS* — A PRODUCT TO BE CONSUMED. I NEED TO FIND A BETTER WAY TO LIBERATE THE CURRICULUM.

I DON'T WANT TO FOLLOW MANDATORY GUIDELINES. I WANT TO FREE MYSELF FROM EASY ANSWERS AND INTELLECTUAL CLAUSTROPHOBIA.

SO HERE'S MY DILEMMA: I NEED TO RECONCILE TWO OPPOSING IDEALS WITHIN A LIMITED SPACE.

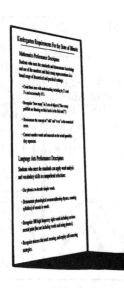

I DON'T WANT TO BOW DOWN TO THE ALMIGHTY LESSON PLAN, AND I DON'T WANT TO LOSE THE IMPORTANCE OF HAVING A TEACHER IN THE CLASSROOM WHO IS A THINKING, FEELING, UNIQUE INDIVIDUAL.

IT IS A FOOL'S ERRAND TO SEARCH FOR A TEACHER-PROOF CURRICULUM. IN SOME WAYS EVERY STUDENT, EVERY TEACHER IS AN ENTIRE UNIVERSE, AND IT'S THE RELATIONSHIP, THE INTERACTION, THAT MAKES LEARNING COME TO LIFE.

LET'S GO EXPLORING ONCE MORE, AND LEARN HOW SOME OTHER FOLKS WORK THE GUTTERS BETWEEN DEMAND AND DESIRE.

ALICE JEFFERSON TEACHES 4TH GRADE IN A CITY SCHOOL.

EVERY YEAR SHE DOES A SUSTAINED STUDY ON A TOPIC SHE KNOWS NOTHING ABOUT.

THAT'S NOT TOO DIFFICULT, SINCE I KNOW NOTHING ABOUT SO MANY THINGS!

SHE CHOOSES LARGE AND AVAILABLE TOPICS LIKE "WHALES," "QUILTING," OR "PAPER," AND PROVIDES SPACE ON A BOOK SHELF AND AN ACTIVITY TABLE DEVOTED TO THIS SPECIAL STUDY.

WHATEVER TOPIC ALICE CHOOSES SEEMS SUDDENLY TO BE EVERYWHERE. OF COURSE, IT WAS THERE ALL THE TIME, BUT CONSCIOUS FOCUS BRINGS IT FRONT AND CENTER.

ALICE SAYS THE SPECIAL TOPICS PLAN KEEPS HER ALIVE AS A TEACHER — ENGAGED, INTELLECTUALLY CURIOUS, ALWAYS LEARNING. HER OWN ENERGY SPARKS UP HER STUDENTS, AS WELL. NEW DISCOVERIES AND EXPERIENCES ARE DRAWN INTO THE VORTEX AND FUEL FURTHER WORK.

SHE HAS OVERTHROWN THE I-KNOW-YOU-DON'T-KNOW STANCE, AND CREATED AN ETHOS OF COLLECTIVE INQUIRY — STUDENTS AND TEACHERS SHOULDER TO SHOULDER INTO THE UNKNOWN.

MEREDITH MCMONIGLE WAS RYAN'S HIGH SCHOOL HISTORY TEACHER.

SHE USED A REQUIRED TEXT AND MADE IT CLEAR TO ALL THAT IT *WAS* REQUIRED, BUT SHE TOOK ANOTHER STEP: EACH UNIT WAS ENHANCED WITH ALTERNATIVE TEXTS, AS WELL AS ART, POETRY, AND FICTION THAT DEFINED THE ERA.

ON THE SUBJECT OF THE ATOMIC BOMBINGS OF HIROSHIMA AND NAGASAKI, THE STANDARD TEXTBOOK PRESENTS THE HEROIC AND STEADY ACTIONS OF PRESIDENT TRUMAN AS HE DROPPED THE BIG ONE AND BESEECHED GOD TO GUIDE HIM SO HE MAY USE THE BOMB "IN HIS WAYS AND FOR HIS PURPOSES."

HOWARD ZINN'S *A PEOPLE'S HISTORY OF THE UNITED STATES*, KEIJI NAKAZAWA'S MANGA SERIES *BAREFOOT GEN*, AND DOCUMENTARY FILMS LIKE *ATOMIC CAFÉ* REVEAL THE UNITED STATES AS A NATION INTENT ON DEMONSTRATING ITS NEW WEAPON, AND A JAPANESE CITIZENRY DECIMATED AS A CONSEQUENCE.

SHE WANTED HER CLASS TO EXAMINE THE CONTRAST BETWEEN TEXTS. THIS PROVIDED A LESSON ABOUT THE SUBJECTIVITY OF HISTORY, AND A BROADER LIFE-LESSON ABOUT CULTURAL AGENDAS AND THE NEED TO ALWAYS QUESTION PERSPECTIVE, STANDPOINT, AND AUTHORSHIP.

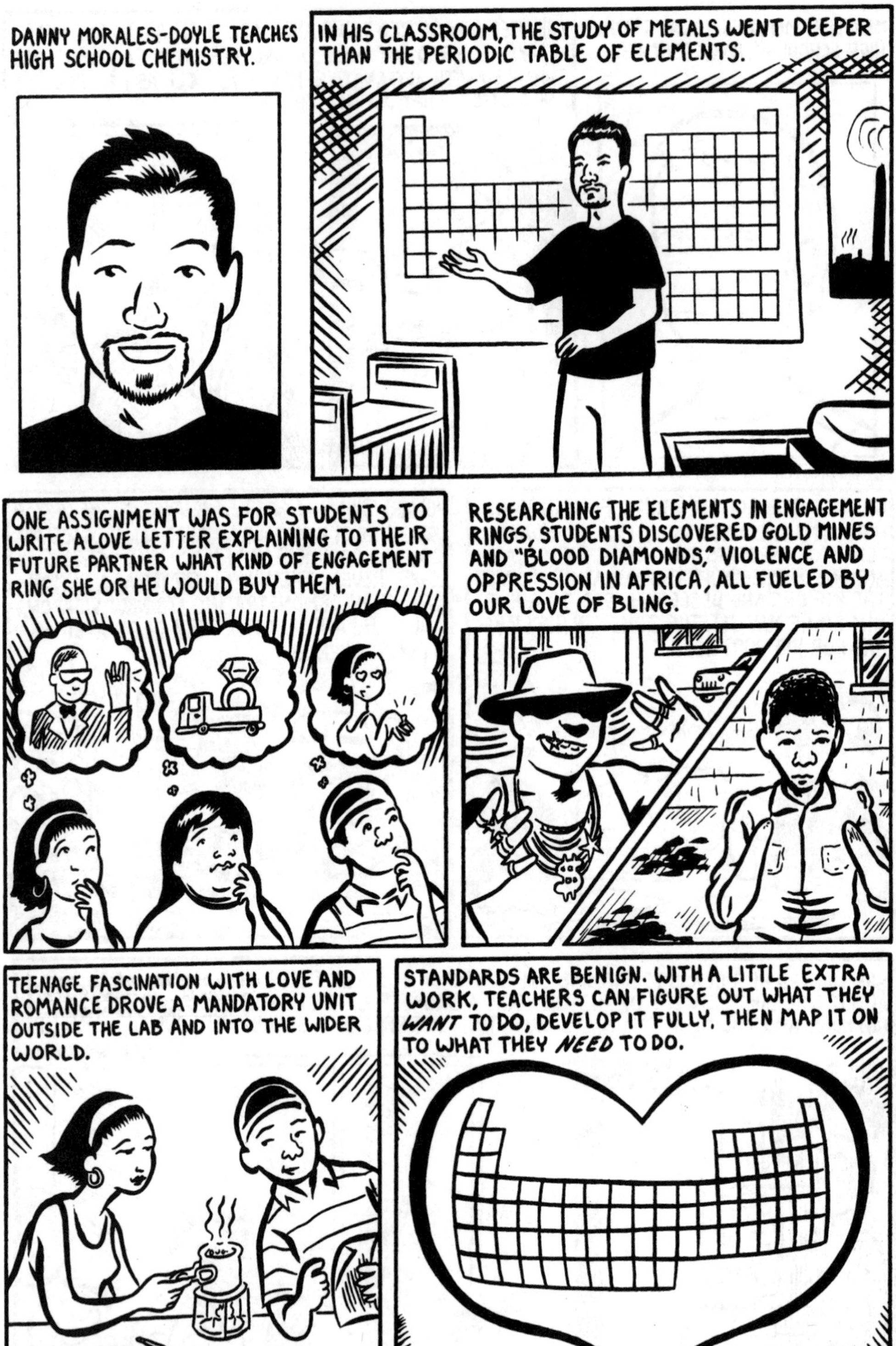
DANNY MORALES-DOYLE TEACHES HIGH SCHOOL CHEMISTRY.
IN HIS CLASSROOM, THE STUDY OF METALS WENT DEEPER THAN THE PERIODIC TABLE OF ELEMENTS.
ONE ASSIGNMENT WAS FOR STUDENTS TO WRITE A LOVE LETTER EXPLAINING TO THEIR FUTURE PARTNER WHAT KIND OF ENGAGEMENT RING SHE OR HE WOULD BUY THEM.
RESEARCHING THE ELEMENTS IN ENGAGEMENT RINGS, STUDENTS DISCOVERED GOLD MINES AND "BLOOD DIAMONDS," VIOLENCE AND OPPRESSION IN AFRICA, ALL FUELED BY OUR LOVE OF BLING.
TEENAGE FASCINATION WITH LOVE AND ROMANCE DROVE A MANDATORY UNIT OUTSIDE THE LAB AND INTO THE WIDER WORLD.
STANDARDS ARE BENIGN. WITH A LITTLE EXTRA WORK, TEACHERS CAN FIGURE OUT WHAT THEY *WANT* TO DO, DEVELOP IT FULLY, THEN MAP IT ON TO WHAT THEY *NEED* TO DO.

SUE HUBBELL ISN'T A TEACHER AT ALL. SHE'S A BEEKEEPER. BUT HER JOURNALS CONTAIN INSIGHTS WE CAN USE.

Beekeepers are an opinionated lot, each sure that his methods alone are the "proper ones". When I first began keeping bees, the diversity of passionately held opinions bewildered me, but now that I have hives in locations scattered over a thousand-square-mile area I think I understand it.

Frosts come earlier in some places...

In others, spring comes later.

Rainfall is not the same. The soils, and the flowering plants they support, are unlike.

I have learned that as a result of these variations I must keep the bees variously. Most people who keep bees have only a few hives, and all in one place. They find it difficult to understand why practices that have proved successful for them do not work for others. But I have learned that I must treat the bees in one yard quite differently from the way I do those even thirty miles away.

The thing to do, I have discovered, is to learn from the bees themselves.

EACH OF YOU IS REQUIRED TO WRITE A COMPLETE SENTENCE ABOUT YOUR EXPERIENCE HERE IN THE PARK.

WHAT DO YOU SEE? WHAT DO YOU SMELL? WHAT DO YOU HEAR? WHAT DO YOU FEEL?

IT'S SO MUCH! BIGGER THAN TV EVEN! I DON'T KNOW WHERE TO BEGIN...

THAT'S THE BEAUTY OF IT.

6
KEEPING TRACK

THE ROOT OF THE WORD "EVALUATION" IS "VALUE," AND
AUTHENTIC ASSESSMENT INCLUDES UNDERSTANDING WHAT
STUDENTS VALUE AND BUILDING FROM THERE. STUDENTS
NEED TO KNOW THAT THEIR PRESENCE IN THE CLASSROOM
IS BOTH VALUED AND VALUABLE. AUTHENTIC ASSESSMENT
IS INSIDE-OUT RATHER THAN OUTSIDE-IN. IT IS AN ATTEMPT
TO GET AWAY FROM SORTING A MASS OF STUDENTS AND
CLOSER TO THE TEACHER'S QUESTION: "GIVEN WHAT I KNOW
NOW, HOW SHOULD I TEACH THIS PARTICULAR STUDENT?"

THE KIDS ARE DOWN THE HALL TAKING THEIR STANDARDIZED TESTS...

I HOPE THEY GET BACK SOON... WE'VE GOT LOTS OF EXCITING THINGS GOING ON IN THE CLASSROOM.

PLUS, I'M LONELY

QUINN! HI, QUINN!

I FINISHED FIRST!

I CAN SEE THAT. HOW DID IT GO?

I DUNNO... FINE, I GUESS...

DID YOU LEARN ANYTHING?

BILL... IT WAS A TEST...

WELL, TELL ME ABOUT IT. HOW DID IT WORK? WHAT DID YOU DO?

UM... I THINK YOU JUST TELL THE PEOPLE WHAT THEY WANT TO KNOW.

THE MOST RECENT STANDARDIZED TEST I TOOK WAS THE BASIC SKILLS TEST FOR A TEACHING CERTIFICATE. A GROUP OF US ASPIRING TEACHERS STOOD LINED UP SINGLE FILE OUTSIDE A HUGE AUDITORIUM, EACH OF US ARMED WITH A BACHELOR'S OR GRADUATE DEGREE IN TEACHING AND A FISTFUL OF #2 PENCILS.

PRECISE DIRECTIONS WERE READ ALOUD TWICE AS WE SHUFFLED INTO OUR SEATS. EFFICIENT-LOOKING MONITORS PATROLLED THE HALL PREPARED TO ESCORT US TO THE BATHROOM, SHARPEN OUR PENCILS, OR SEIZE OUR TEST BOOKLETS IF WE CHEATED. THIS WAS HIGH RITUAL.

ONE LAST HOOP TO JUMP THROUGH... THIS SHOULD BE A CINCH...

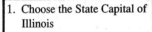

1. Choose the State Capital of Illinois
   A. Chicago
   B. Springfield
   C. Lincoln
   D. Rockford

EASY! B. SPRINGFIELD.

2. Field trip rental fee:
   $240.00   30 students
   Activity fee per student:
   A. $5
   B. $8
   C. $10
   D. $15

LET'S SEE... CANCEL THE ZEROES... B. 8 DOLLARS.

3. An outstanding resource for a study of Thomas Edison is:
   A. Field trip to the electric company
   B. Biography by Neal Baldwin
   C. The US National Park Service
   D. All of the above

HMM...THEY ALL SOUND GOOD TO ME... D.

MAN, THIS IS EASY!

4. Select the correct non-verbal agreement
   A. We are going to dinner later.
   B. We have going to dinner tomorrow.
   C. We be going to dinner this evening.
   D. We will going to dinner after work.

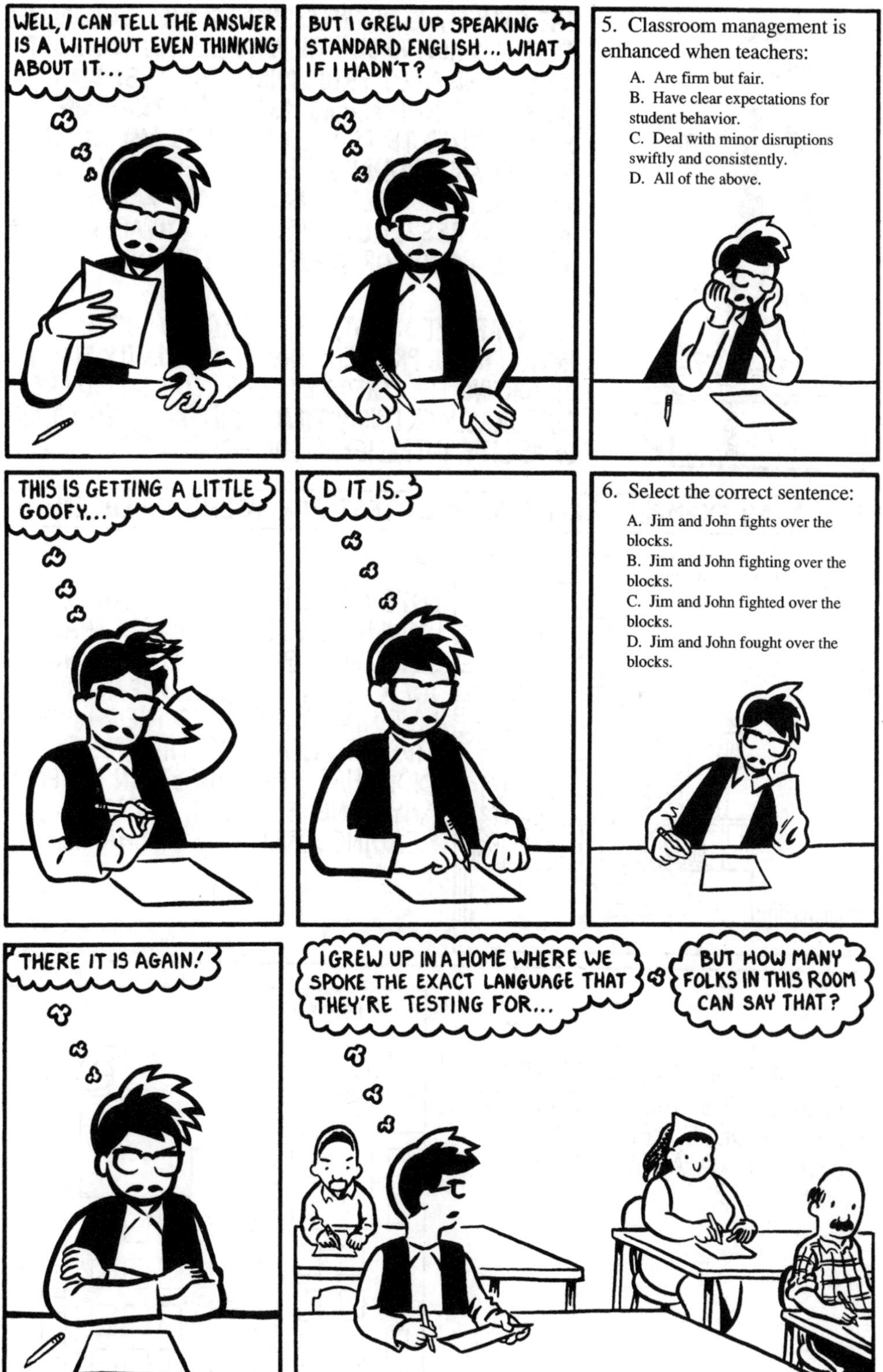
WELL, I CAN TELL THE ANSWER IS A WITHOUT EVEN THINKING ABOUT IT...
BUT I GREW UP SPEAKING STANDARD ENGLISH... WHAT IF I HADN'T?
5. Classroom management is enhanced when teachers:
A. Are firm but fair.
B. Have clear expectations for student behavior.
C. Deal with minor disruptions swiftly and consistently.
D. All of the above.
THIS IS GETTING A LITTLE GOOFY...
D IT IS.
6. Select the correct sentence:
A. Jim and John fights over the blocks.
B. Jim and John fighting over the blocks.
C. Jim and John fighted over the blocks.
D. Jim and John fought over the blocks.
THERE IT IS AGAIN!
I GREW UP IN A HOME WHERE WE SPOKE THE EXACT LANGUAGE THAT THEY'RE TESTING FOR...
BUT HOW MANY FOLKS IN THIS ROOM CAN SAY THAT?

THE ONLY THING QUINN LEARNED FROM HIS STANDARDIZED TEST WAS HOW TO GIVE THE ANSWERS THEY WANT, BUT I LEARNED A LOT FROM MINE. THE TEST WAS DEMEANING TO TEACHING AND TO THE TEST-TAKERS. STANDARDIZED TESTS HOLD TEACHERS AND SCHOOLS ACCOUNTABLE TO ONLY A FEW OF THEIR MANY GOALS. I MAY GET A PERFECT SCORE OR I MAY FAIL, BUT NEITHER RESULT COULD POSSIBLY EXPLAIN WHETHER I'LL BE A GOOD OR A ROTTEN TEACHER.

STANDARDIZED TESTS ARE PLAGUED WITH INTRACTABLE PROBLEMS, THEY'RE INHERENTLY BIASED, DISTORTING THE PERFORMANCE OF PEOPLE WHO ARE CULTURALLY OR LINGUISTICALLY DIFFERENT, REGARDLESS OF ABILITY, INTELLIGENCE, OR ACHIEVEMENT.

HERE'S AN EXAMPLE FROM A READING TEST FOR YOUNG CHILDREN:

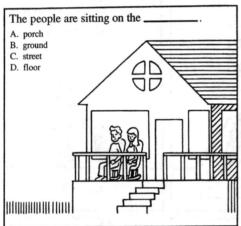

The people are sitting on the _____.
A. porch
B. ground
C. street
D. floor

LOTS OF 1ST-GRADERS I KNOW WOULD BE ABLE TO READ THAT SENTENCE, BUT WOULD HAVE NO IDEA WHAT PORCHES ARE, HAVING LIVED IN APARTMENTS THEIR WHOLE LIVES. TO CLAIM, AS THIS TEST DID, THAT THE QUESTION REVEALS ANYTHING SENSIBLE ABOUT READING ABILITY IS A SHAM.

ASSUME A DIFFERENT CULTURAL STANCE. HOW WOULD EVEN THE MOST WIDELY READ KIDS IN RURAL IOWA ANSWER *THIS* QUESTION?

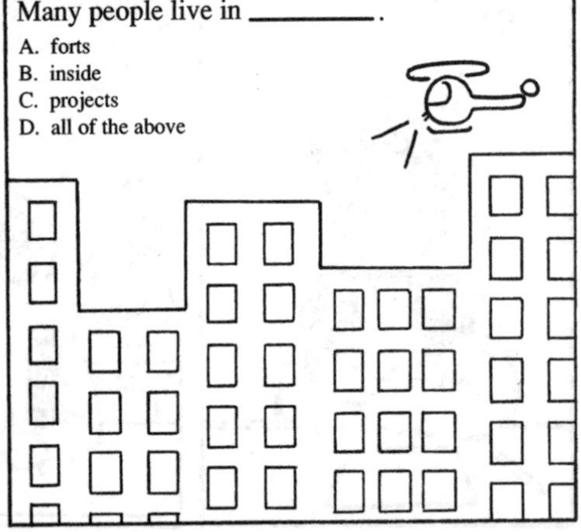

Many people live in _____.
A. forts
B. inside
C. projects
D. all of the above

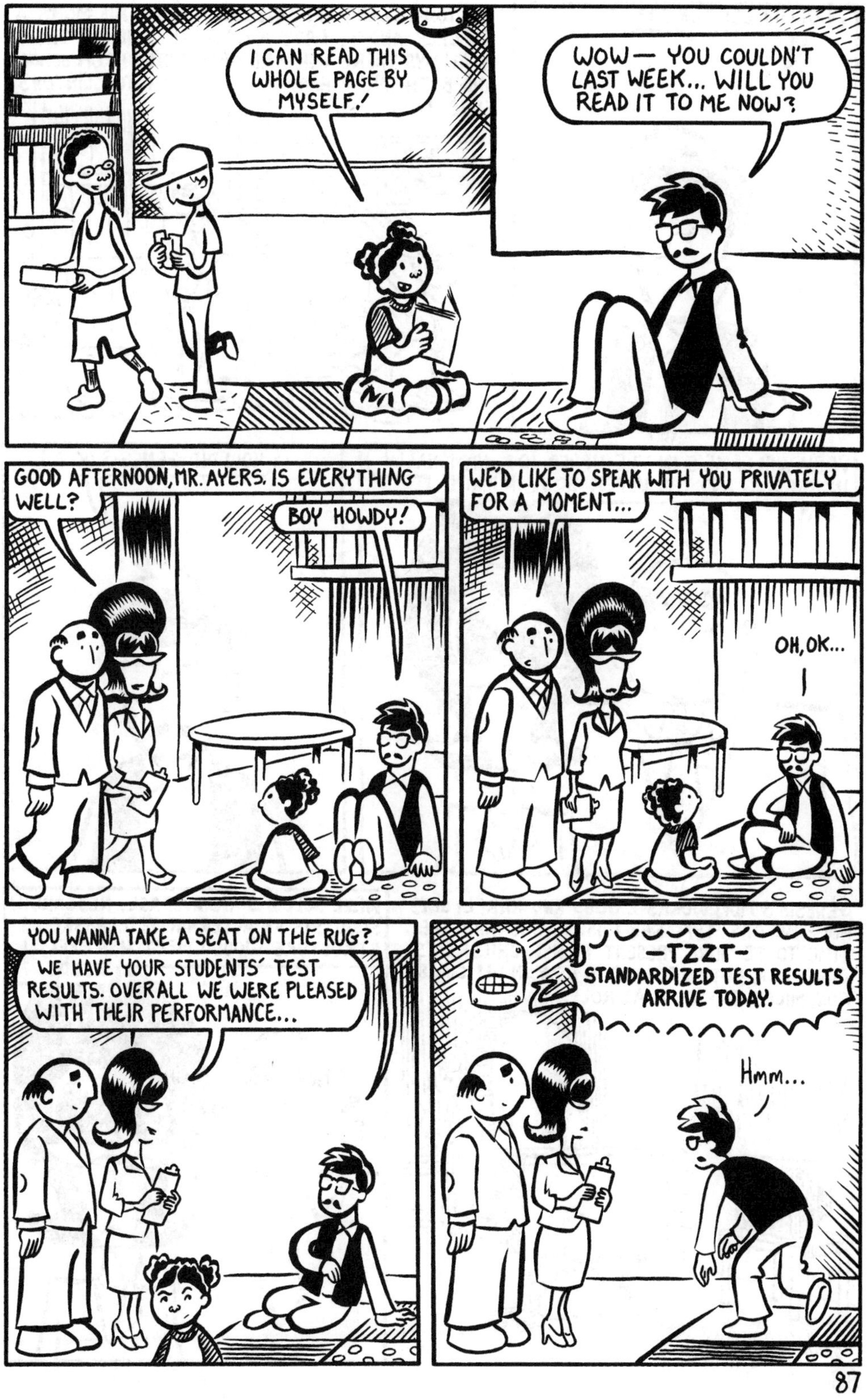
I CAN READ THIS WHOLE PAGE BY MYSELF!
WOW— YOU COULDN'T LAST WEEK... WILL YOU READ IT TO ME NOW?
GOOD AFTERNOON, MR. AYERS. IS EVERYTHING WELL?
BOY HOWDY!
WE'D LIKE TO SPEAK WITH YOU PRIVATELY FOR A MOMENT...
OH, OK...
YOU WANNA TAKE A SEAT ON THE RUG?
WE HAVE YOUR STUDENTS' TEST RESULTS. OVERALL WE WERE PLEASED WITH THEIR PERFORMANCE...
-TZZT-
STANDARDIZED TEST RESULTS ARRIVE TODAY.
Hmm...

HOW DID CLINTON DO?

CLINTON'S FOLKS ARE INTELLECTUALS — HIS MOM'S A TEACHER AND HIS DAD'S A MUSICIAN. ONE OF THEM IS ALWAYS THERE WHEN HE GETS HOME FROM SCHOOL, AND BOTH TAKE A HANDS-ON APPROACH TO CLINTON'S EDUCATION.

VERY WELL. HE'S IN THE UPPER 10% NATIONALLY IN READING AND THE UPPER 30% IN MATH.

HOW DID GENESIS DO?

GENESIS'S MOM WORKS 2 JOBS AND RARELY GETS HOME BEFORE 9 PM. SHE WISHES SHE HAD THE TIME TO BE MORE PRESENT IN HER CHILDREN'S EDUCATION, BUT OFTEN HAS TO RELY ON HER OLDEST SON, MILES, TO FILL THAT ROLE.

WELL BELOW STATE AVERAGE, RESEARCH SUGGESTS AN ALTERNATIVE CLASSROOM STRUCTURE WOULD MEET HER SPECIAL NEEDS...

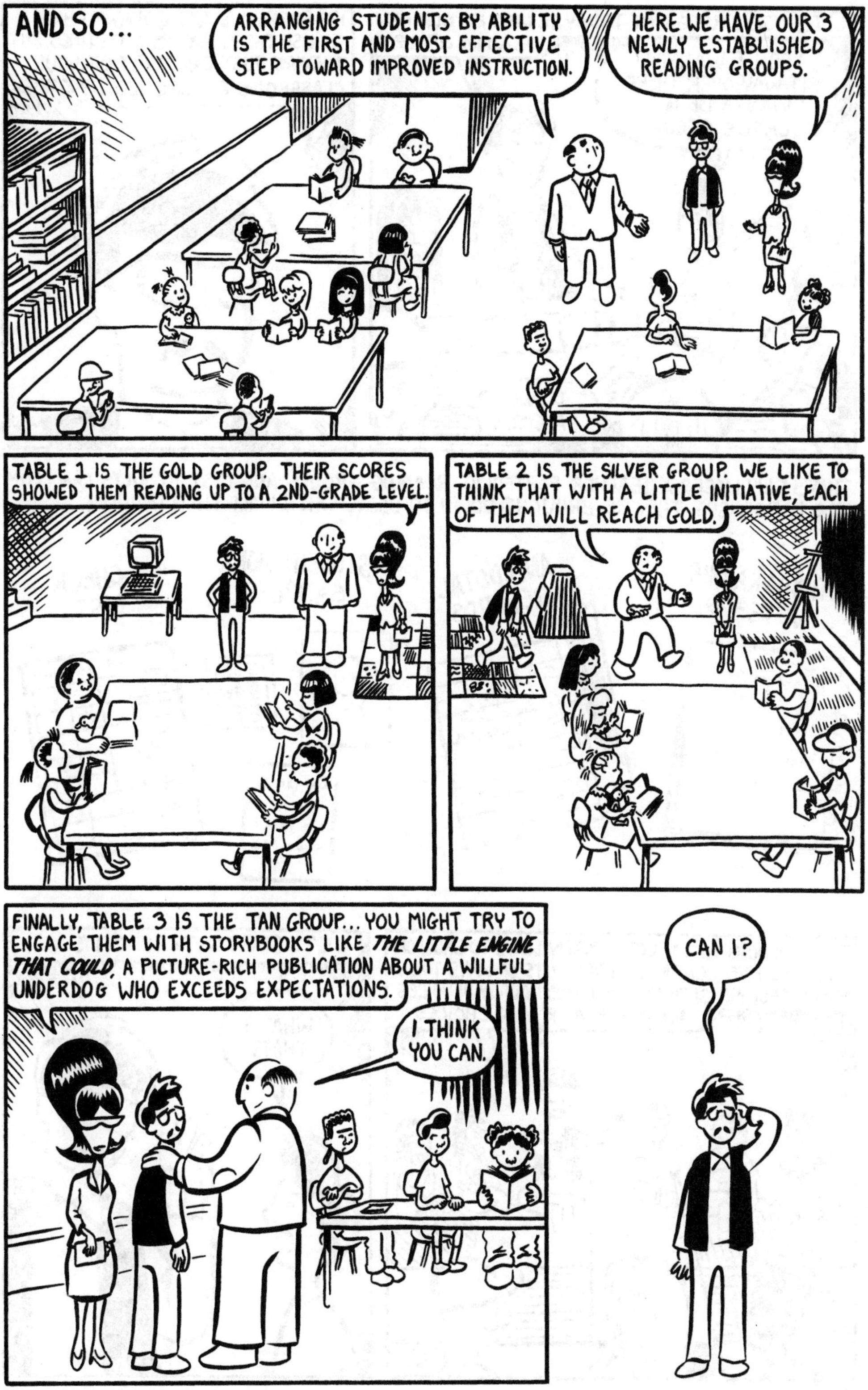
AND SO...
ARRANGING STUDENTS BY ABILITY IS THE FIRST AND MOST EFFECTIVE STEP TOWARD IMPROVED INSTRUCTION.
HERE WE HAVE OUR 3 NEWLY ESTABLISHED READING GROUPS.
TABLE 1 IS THE GOLD GROUP. THEIR SCORES SHOWED THEM READING UP TO A 2ND-GRADE LEVEL.
TABLE 2 IS THE SILVER GROUP. WE LIKE TO THINK THAT WITH A LITTLE INITIATIVE, EACH OF THEM WILL REACH GOLD.
FINALLY, TABLE 3 IS THE TAN GROUP... YOU MIGHT TRY TO ENGAGE THEM WITH STORYBOOKS LIKE *THE LITTLE ENGINE THAT COULD*, A PICTURE-RICH PUBLICATION ABOUT A WILLFUL UNDERDOG WHO EXCEEDS EXPECTATIONS.
I THINK YOU CAN.
CAN I?

THAT'S WHY I KEEP A TEACHER PORTFOLIO. READING GROUPS AND TEST RESULTS CAN LOOM TOO LARGE, BUT THEY'RE BROUGHT DOWN TO SCALE WHEN I MIX THEM IN WITH...

PERFORMANCES CAN BE ANYTHING WE WORK ON TO MAKE A PRESENTATION TO AN AUDIENCE, LIKE THE STORY THEATER WE DID FOR THE WHOLE SCHOOL LAST MONTH. YOU WORKED HARD BECAUSE YOU HAD AN AUDIENCE BEYOND THE GRADEBOOK...

PROJECTS ARE SPECIAL INTERESTS THAT WE FOCUS ON OVER TIME, LIKE OUR BOARD GAMES PROJECT WHERE TEAMS INVENTED GAMES, OR OUR MAPPING THE NEIGHBORHOOD PROJECT, OR OUR HEALTHY GARDEN PROJECT, OR OUR FAMILY TREES.

PORTFOLIOS ARE RIGOROUS, DETAILED COLLECTIONS OF EACH STUDENT'S WORK THUS FAR: PAINTING FILES AND JOURNALS, JOB CHARTS AND RECORDS OF CLASSROOM SERVICE, ESSAYS AND COMICS AND PHOTOGRAPHS.

IT'S IMPORTANT FOR ME TO KNOW WHERE EACH OF YOU IS LEARNING-WISE, BUT SINCE EACH OF YOU LEARNS DIFFERENTLY, WE'LL TRY A LOT OF DIFFERENT THINGS...

AND SINCE WE *ARE* KEEPING THE READING GROUPS, LET'S CHANGE THE TAN GROUP TO BRONZE. WHY THE MOST CHALLENGED READERS SHOULD BE DEPRIVED OF PRECIOUS METALS, I DO NOT KNOW...

I WANT YOU TO EXPLORE AND STRETCH AND INVESTIGATE AND WONDER AND WORK AND HAVE A GOOD TIME AND READ AND WRITE AND SOLVE PROBLEMS.

WE'VE ALL GOT OUR WORK CUT OUT FOR US. DON'T WORRY ABOUT GROUPS AND TESTS — WE'VE GOT TOO MUCH TO DO. LET'S SHAKE THINGS UP!

SHAKE IT!

SHAKE IT, BABY!

SHAKE SHAKE SHAKE

SHAKE IT UP!

7
THE MYSTERY OF TEACHING

THE WORK OF A TEACHER — EXHAUSTING, COMPLEX, IDIOSYNCRATIC, NEVER TWICE THE SAME — IS, AT HEART, AN INTELLECTUAL AND ETHICAL ENTERPRISE. TEACHING IS THE VOCATION OF VOCATIONS, A CALLING THAT SHEPHERDS A MULTITUDE OF OTHER CALLINGS. IT IS AN ACTIVITY THAT IS INTENSELY PRACTICAL AND YET TRANSCENDENT, BRUTALLY MATTER-OF-FACT AND YET FUNDAMENTALLY A CREATIVE ACT. THE IMMENSE JOURNEY OF A TEACHER BEGINS IN CHALLENGE AND IS NEVER FAR FROM MYSTERY.

IT MEANS "TO TAKE AWAY."

SO WHEN WE SAY "SUBTRACT," OR "MINUS," IT MEANS TO TAKE AWAY.

Ooooh...

SO: HOW MANY RODS DO YOU HAVE?

1, 2, 3...
11 RODS.

AND WHAT DO YOU GET WHEN YOU TAKE 3 AWAY?

HMM...
1, 2, 3...

NOW THERE ARE 8 RODS.

RIGHT! AND IF YOU SUBTRACT 4 MORE?

...4 RODS NOW.

EXACTLY. AND THAT'S HOW SUBTRACTION WORKS.

I CAN DO IT NOW.

I'M SO PROUD OF YOU!

DOES ANYONE ELSE NEED HELP WITH SUBTRACTION?

I DO!

OK, SO: HOW MANY RODS DO YOU HAVE?

I DUNNO.

WHY DON'T YOU COUNT THEM?

WHY?

SO YOU KNOW HOW MANY YOU'RE SUBTRACTING FROM.

WHAT'S THAT?

IT MEANS "TO TAKE AWAY."

I WANNA PLAY CHECKERS.

I'LL PLAY CHECKERS WITH YOU AFTER WE LEARN SUBTRACTION...

WHAT'S THAT?

...LOOK, THERE ARE 9 RODS HERE, RIGHT?

IF YOU SAY SO...

SO WHAT DO WE GET WHEN WE TAKE 3 AWAY?

WE GET TO PLAY CHECKERS!

95

THE RENOWNED RUSSIAN DIRECTOR STANISLAVSKY ARGUED 3 COMMON BELIEFS ABOUT ACTING THAT STOOD IN THE WAY OF GREATNESS.

1. "ACTING IS ESSENTIALLY MECHANICAL." SAY YOUR LINES, HIT YOUR SPOTS, AND VOILA! YOU'RE AN ACTOR.

GREAT ACTORS ENGAGE AN AUDIENCE, INTERACT, AND DRAW ENERGY AND INSPIRATION FROM THE RELATIONSHIP.

2. "A ROLE CAN BE FINISHED IN SOME PERFECT OR FINAL SENSE." ONCE YOU MASTER LADY MACBETH, YOU CAN PLAY HER ON AUTOMATIC PILOT FOREVER.

GREAT ACTORS REALIZE A PART IS NEVER DONE, BUT MUST BE LEARNED ANEW — GREAT ACTING IS IN SEARCH OF BETTER ACTING.

3. "ACTING IS EXTERNAL." YOU CAN ACT ANGRY WITHOUT EVER FEELING ANGER, PLAY A BROKEN HEARTED LOVER WITHOUT KNOWING LOVE OR LOSS.

GREAT ACTORS FIND A SEED OF AUTHENTICITY TO MOVE FROM CARICATURE TO COMPLEX, LIVING HUMAN BEINGS.

THESE PRINCIPLES HAVE A UNIVERSALITY; STANISLAVSKY COULD WELL BE ADVISING TEACHERS.

GREATNESS IN TEACHING, TOO, REQUIRES A SERIOUS ENCOUNTER WITH AUTOBIOGRAPHY. WHO ARE YOU? HOW DID YOU COME TO TAKE ON YOUR VIEWS AND OUTLOOKS? WHAT WAS IT LIKE FOR YOU TO BE 6? WHERE ARE YOU HEADING? OF ALL THE KNOWLEDGE TEACHERS NEED TO DRAW ON, SELF-KNOWLEDGE IS MOST IMPORTANT.

GREATNESS IN TEACHING REQUIRES GETTING OVER THE NOTION THAT IT'S SETS OF TECHNIQUES OR METHODS...LOTS OF FOLKS WRITE ADEQUATE LESSON PLANS, KEEP ORDER, DELIVER INSTRUCTION— AND ARE LOUSY TEACHERS.

GREATNESS IN TEACHING ENGAGES STUDENTS, INTERACTS WITH THEM, DRAWS ENERGY AND DIRECTION FROM THEM, AND OFFERS REASONS TO PLUNGE INTO CLASSROOM LIFE.

GREATNESS IN TEACHING IS ALWAYS IN PURSUIT OF THE NEXT CHALLENGE, THE NEXT ENCOUNTER... GREATNESS DEMANDS AN OPENNESS TO THE NEW AND THE UNIQUE. FOR GREAT TEACHERS, IT MUST ALWAYS BE "HERE I GO AGAIN."

THERE ARE HUNDREDS OF THINGS TEACHERS NEED TO KNOW IN ORDER TO ACHIEVE GREATNESS, MANY OF WHICH ARE DISCOVERED AS NEEDED.

CREATIVE INSUBORDINATION

-TZZT- IT'S TIME TO RECITE THE STAR-SPANGLED BANNER.

I'D HAD ENOUGH. WHEN THE KIDS LEFT FOR RECESS, I TOOK THE FACE OFF THE INTERCOM AND CLIPPED THE WIRES.

AFTER REASSEMBLING IT, I REPORTED THAT IT HAD MYSTERIOUSLY BROKEN. PEACE AND QUIET AT LAST!

FINDING ALLIES

TEACHING IS OFTEN ISOLATED AND ISOLATING.

OUTSTANDING TEACHING OFTEN GOES AGAINST THE GRAIN, AND IS BEST ACCOMPLISHED WITH ALLIES.

LEARNING TO FORM ALLIANCES WITH SUPPORTERS, PARENTS, FRIENDS, CO-CONSPIRATORS, CAN BE LIFE SAVING.

CRITICISM

ONCE A COLLEAGUE OF MINE REPRIMANDED A STUDENT BY THREATENING TO CUT OFF HER PONY TAIL.

I INTERVENED, COMFORTED THE CHILD, AND PURSUED A COMPLAINT DESPITE REMARKABLE PEER RESISTANCE.

IF TEACHERS ARE NEVER CRITICAL, THEY NEVER HAVE TO TEST THEIR DEEPEST BELIEFS AND VALUES, AND CAN BECOME THE TEACHERS THEY ONCE DESPISED.

SELF-CRITICISM

THE MYSTERY OF TEACHING KEEPS ME ON MY TOES.

IF TEACHERS ARE NEVER SELF-CRITICAL, THEY WILL BECOME DOGMATIC, LOSING THEIR CAPACITY FOR RENEWAL AND GROWTH.

IF THEY'RE *TOO* SELF-CRITICAL, THEY BECOME POWERLESS AND TIMID. BALANCE AND CLARITY IS KEY.

LEARNING FROM YOUR OWN EXPERIENCE

FOR YEARS I'D BEEN COACHING PARENTS THROUGH SEPARATION ANXIETY ON THE FIRST DAY OF SCHOOL.

WHEN WE SENT OUR FIRST CHILD TO HIS FIRST DAY OF SCHOOL, I WAS INCONSOLABLE.

TEACHERS ARE ENCOURAGED TO DEVELOP A PROFESSIONAL STANCE THAT IS OUTSIDE THEIR OWN EXPERIENCE. GOOD TEACHING REQUIRES AUDACITY, BUT ALSO HUMILITY.

AUTHENTIC FRIENDSHIP

EVERY TEACHER WANTS TO BE WELL-LIKED, BUT THE IDEAL OF STUDENT FRIENDSHIPS CAN BE A TRAP.

EASY FRIENDSHIPS WITH STUDENTS CAN BLUR LINES OF RESPONSIBILITY.

AUTHENTIC FRIENDSHIP IS A MATTER OF SOLIDARITY BETWEEN HUMAN BEINGS, AND SOLIDARITY MEANS CRITICISM AS WELL AS ACCEPTANCE.

LINKING CONSCIOUSNESS TO CONDUCT

MANY TEACHERS IMAGINE THEIR CLASSROOMS AS SAFE HAVENS, WALLED OFF FROM THE OUTSIDE WORLD AND ALL ITS TROUBLES.

CRACKS IN THE WALL ARE INEVITABLE. STUDENTS SPEND MOST OF THEIR TIME IN THE LARGER WORLD, AND ARE BOUND TO BRING IT WITH THEM TO CLASS.

TEACHING TOWARD SOMETHING BETTER REQUIRES INVOLVEMENT IN FAMILIES, COMMUNITIES, NEIGHBORHOODS, SOCIETY.

BALANCE AND CLARITY

THERE ARE THOUSANDS OF CREATIVE IDEAS FOR DYNAMIC TEACHING.

TEACHERS ARE TYPICALLY TRAPPED IN THE ROLE OF PASSIVE RECIPIENTS OF IDEAS RATHER THAN ACTIVE CREATORS.

THE STRUGGLE IS NOT TO STOCKPILE IDEAS, BUT TO FIND THE CORE VALUES THAT DEFINE CLASSROOM LIFE.

GREAT TEACHING IS THE FUNDAMENTAL ELEMENT IN EVERY GOOD SCHOOL.

GOOD SCHOOLS ARE GEARED TOWARD CONTINUOUS IMPROVEMENT.

GOOD SCHOOLS ARE POWERED BY CORE VALUES THAT ARE EXPLICIT, APPARENT, AND EMBODIED IN DAILY LIFE.

GOOD SCHOOLS HAVE HIGH EXPECTATIONS FOR ALL LEARNERS. STUDENTS FEEL NOURISHED AND CHALLENGED IN THE SAME GESTURE.

GOOD SCHOOLS ARE ALWAYS UNIQUE: EACH IS THE CREATION OF PARTICULAR PEOPLE WORKING TO BRING THEIR VISION TO LIFE IN CLASSROOMS.

GOOD SCHOOLS ARE PLACES WHERE LOTS OF GOOD TEACHERS HAVE BEEN GATHERED TOGETHER AND ALLOWED TO TEACH.

DAVE STOVALL AND KATIE HOGAN ARE 2 OF THE FOUNDING TEACHERS AT LAWNDALE LITTLE VILLAGE, A PUBLIC HIGH SCHOOL IN CHICAGO.

GOOD SCHOOLS ARE PLACES WHERE STUDENTS COME TO BELIEVE IN THEIR OWN CAPACITY TO CHANGE THE WORLD.

GOOD SCHOOLS ARE PLACES WHERE TEACHERS AND KIDS ALIKE CAN BE BOTH GOOFY AND SERIOUS.

GOOD SCHOOLS ARE PLACES WHERE EDUCATION IS UNDERSTOOD TO BE A MATTER OF LIFE AND DEATH.

GOOD SCHOOLS ARE PLACES WHERE STUDENTS FEEL IT'S OK TO CRY IN A CLASSROOM.

GOOD SCHOOLS ARE PLACES WHERE STUDENTS ARE VALUED.

HEY, MARCUS

HEY, MS. HOGAN

IT'S A SACRED PLACE, THIS SCHOOL. IT WAS A DREAM BEFORE IT WAS A REALITY, AND THE WOMEN WHOSE SACRIFICE BROUGHT IT TO LIFE MUST BE HONORED.

SHE'S REFERRING TO THE UNIQUE CIRCUMSTANCES AND DIRECT ACTIONS THAT LED TO THE CREATION OF THE SCHOOL.

LITTLE VILLAGE IS THE HEART OF CHICAGO'S LARGEST LATINO IMMIGRANT COMMUNITY.

BIENVENIDOS A LITTLE VILLAGE

SCHOOLS HERE WERE CHRONICALLY OVERCROWDED AND UNDER-RESOURCED.

FOR YEARS, PARENTS IN THE COMMUNITY RELENTLESSLY PRESSED THE CITY TO TAKE ACTION.

102

FINALLY THE CITY PROMISED THAT A NEW HIGH SCHOOL WOULD BE BUILT.

A SITE WAS SELECTED, BUT OVER TIME THE EMPTY LOT SHOWED NOTHING MORE THAN AN EMPTY PROMISE.

WHEN THE CITY ANNOUNCED THAT THERE WAS "NO MONEY IN THIS YEAR'S BUDGET," 14 MOTHERS AND GRANDMOTHERS GATHERED AT THE SITE AND DECLARED A HUNGER STRIKE UNTIL THE PROMISE WAS FULFILLED.

ON THE 19TH DAY OF THE HUNGER STRIKE, THE CHICAGO PUBLIC SCHOOLS LEADER ANNOUNCED THAT THE MONEY WAS FOUND. LITTLE VILLAGE WOULD HAVE ITS SCHOOL!

PARENTS, COMMUNITY MEMBERS, AND EDUCATORS LIKE KATIE AND DAVE CAME TOGETHER TO IMAGINE AND DESIGN THE SCHOOL OF THEIR DREAMS...

THE NEIGHBORING COMMUNITY OF NORTH LAWNDALE, A PREDOMINANTLY AFRICAN-AMERICAN AREA WITH A RICH HISTORY OF INVOLVEMENT IN THE CIVIL RIGHTS MOVEMENT, JOINED THE CAUSE.

THE DESIGN TEAM, NOW FULLY ASSEMBLED, TOOK ITS CHARGE TO HEART: THEY TALKED TO ARCHITECTS AND CURRICULUM SPECIALISTS, SCHOOL LEADERS AND RESEARCHERS, AND TOURED SCHOOLS ALL OVER CHICAGOLAND.

LAWNDALE LITTLE VILLAGE HIGH SCHOOL EMBODIES THE PRIORITIES THEY ESTABLISHED.

PARENTS ARE CRITICAL TO THE FORM AND FUNCTION OF THIS PLACE. MORE THAN "VALUABLE" OR "RESPECTED" THEY'RE *CRITICAL*.

LOOK AT OUR HISTORY. PARENTS BUILT THIS SCHOOL. THEY'RE LEADERS AND ELDERS. WE'RE HERE BECAUSE OF THEM AND WE CAN'T DO IT WITHOUT THEM. WE'RE ALLIES.

THE RELATIONSHIP BETWEEN THE SCHOOL AND NEIGHBORHOODS IS NOURISHED AND VALUED. EVERY SUMMER, TEACHERS DO HOME VISITS TO BREAK DOWN THE IDEA THAT WE LIVE IN ENTIRELY SEPARATE AND IMPENETRABLE WORLDS.

HI, I'M DAVE! I'LL BE TEACHING YOUR KIDS. JUST HERE TO SAY HELLO... IF YOU NEED ANYTHING AS THE SCHOOL YEAR GOES BY, MY CLASSROOM'S ALWAYS OPEN...

THIS IS NEW...

STUDENTS ARE, OF COURSE, AT THE CENTER. EACH STUDENT IS KNOWN AND RECOGNIZED WITHIN THE SCHOOL, AND TEACHERS ARE ABLE TO BUILD AUTHENTIC RELATIONSHIPS WITH THEM.

IN ORDER FOR STUDENTS TO HAVE THEIR RIGHTFUL PLACE, THE DESIGN TEAM DETERMINED THAT THE CAMPUS WOULD BE STRUCTURED AS 4 SMALL SCHOOLS, EACH WITH ITS OWN DISTINCT MISSION STATEMENT.

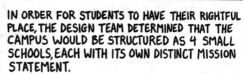

105

WORLD LANGUAGE HIGH SCHOOL TEACHES MULTIPLE LANGUAGES AS THE ENTRY POINT INTO LEARNING ABOUT ALL THE WAYS THAT HUMANS CREATE MEANING AND SIGNIFICANCE.

LANGUAGE UNLOCKS THE WORLD.

INFINITY HIGH SCHOOL FOLLOWS ADVANCED TECHNOLOGY AS A PATHWAY TO INTELLECTUAL CURIOSITY AND ACADEMIC ENGAGEMENT.

GAMES AND GADGETS LEAD STUDENTS TO THE FUTURE.

MULTICULTURAL ARTS HIGH SCHOOL NOURISHES CREATIVITY AND IMAGINATION THROUGH ENGAGEMENT WITH THE VISUAL ARTS, THEATER, MUSIC, AND DANCE.

ART URGES VOYAGES.

SOCIAL JUSTICE HIGH SCHOOL IS BUILT ON RESPECT AND RECOGNITION OF THE FULL HUMANITY OF EACH PERSON, AND POWERED BY IDEAS OF PEACE AND FAIRNESS.

SOCIAL JUSTICE HELPS STUDENTS BELIEVE ANOTHER WORLD IS POSSIBLE.

KATIE AND DAVE TEACH AT SOCIAL JUSTICE HIGH SCHOOL, WHICH IS FOUNDED ON 4 CORE VALUES:

TRUTH AND TRANSPARENCY

WE WILL PRACTICE HONESTY AND AUTHENTICITY IN OUR COMMUNICATION AND RELATIONSHIPS WITH STUDENTS, OUR COMMUNITY, PEERS, AND OURSELVES.

STRUGGLE AND SACRIFICE

OUR STRUGGLE IS AGAINST SYSTEMS OF POWER THAT HAVE BEEN HISTORICALLY USED TO DENY, REGULATE, AND PROHIBIT ACCESS TO THE MOST BASIC HUMAN RIGHTS THAT SHOULD BE GRANTED FREELY TO ALL PEOPLE. WE ACCEPT THE REALITY THAT SUCH STRUGGLE WILL REQUIRE SACRIFICE FROM ALL INVOLVED.

OWNERSHIP AND AGENCY

WE WILL TAKE RESPONSIBILITY AS AGENTS AND CATALYSTS OF CHANGE TO EXPOSE THE TRUTH ABOUT FUNCTIONS OF POWER, UNITE TO INTERRUPT THEIR OPERATIONS, AND OPERATE AS PRODUCERS OF POWER TO MEET THE NEEDS OF THE GREATER COMMUNITY.

COLLECTIVE AND COMMUNITY POWER

WE COMMIT TO A CONSCIOUS EFFORT TO OVERCOME THE INTENDED HISTORICAL OBSTACLES THAT HAVE BEEN DESIGNED TO DISEMPOWER AND DIVIDE OUR COMMUNITIES, AND THEREBY MEET THE NEEDS OF ALL ITS MEMBERS FOR CONTINUAL BETTERMENT AND PROGRESS.

NORTH LAWNDALE AND LITTLE VILLAGE ARE 2 COMMUNITIES — ONE BLACK, ONE LATINO — WITH A HISTORY OF TENSION.

ACKNOWLEDGING THAT TENSION, BREAKING DOWN PREJUDICES, AND FINDING COMMON GROUND IS INGRAINED IN ALL ASPECTS OF THE CURRICULUM.

ENGLISH CLASSES INCLUDE COMPARATIVE ANALYSIS BETWEEN BLACK AND LATINO LITERATURE.

SOCIAL STUDIES CLASSES TEAM UP WITH COMMUNITY ORGANIZATIONS TO EXAMINE ISSUES LIKE EDUCATION, THE ENVIRONMENT, SUSTAINABLE LIVING, YOUTH VIOLENCE, GENTRIFICATION.

MY GOAL IS SIMPLE: I WANT TO ENGAGE FOLKS IN DISCUSSIONS LEADING TO INFORMED DECISIONS ABOUT REALITY... HOW THINGS ARE, HOW THEY MIGHT BE CHANGED.

IF YOU HAVE A STAFF OF FOLKS COMMITTED TO THIS TYPE OF WORK, YOU CAN MAKE IT HAPPEN.

THE STAFF DOESN'T GO IT ALONE—PARENTS HAVE FORMED THEIR OWN LEADERSHIP TEAM IN ORDER TO ACTIVELY PARTICIPATE IN SCHOOL LIFE.

THEIR SESSIONS DON'T FOCUS ON BUDGET OR GRADES... RATHER, THEY INVITE PEOPLE TO TELL THEIR STORIES AND MAKE CONNECTIONS.

THAT IMPULSE TOWARD COMMUNITY COMES RIGHT OUT OF THE SUCCESS OF THE HUNGER STRIKE, THE BELIEF THAT THE CONTRIBUTION OF EACH MAKES THE GROUP STRONGER. IT FLOWS NATURALLY INTO CURRICULUM AND TEACHING AND THE EMBRACING CULTURE OF THE SCHOOL.

SOCIAL JUSTICE IS CERTAINLY ABOUT ACCESS AND EQUITY, BUT IT'S MORE THAN THAT...

IT'S ALSO ABOUT FULL RECOGNITION OF THE UNIQUE QUALITIES OF EACH HUMAN BEING.

MAYRA CERVANTES WAS A QUIET KID, SELDOM NOTICED AND HAPPY WITH A LOW "B" IN KATIE'S JUNIOR ENGLISH CLASS.

KATIE WOULD OFTEN DRAW ATTENTION TO MAYRA'S SUCCESS ON THE CROSS-COUNTRY TEAM, SOMETIMES JOKING THAT THEY SHOULD HAVE A RACE.

ONE DAY MAYRA ACCEPTED THE CHALLENGE, SENDING A SHOCKWAVE THROUGHOUT THE ROOM. SOON, PLANNING THE RACE BECAME A SMALL PART OF EACH CLASS, AN ARDENT ACTIVITY THAT CREATED FOCUSED ATTENTION THROUGHOUT THE PERIOD.

BY THE DAY OF THE GREAT RACE, THE CLASS HAD BECOME A CLOSE-KNIT, SPIRITED, AND COHERENT GROUP, BROUGHT TOGETHER BY COLLECTIVE INTEREST AND ENTHUSIASM.

THE RACE TOOK UP A SINGLE CLASS PERIOD. IT WAS A SMALL PRICE TO PAY FOR THE UNIFICATION OF A GROUP OF YOUNG LEARNERS, WHICH LASTED THE REST OF THE YEAR.

AND AT THE CENTER OF IT ALL, STAR OF THE SHOW, WAS MAYRA.

THERE'S SO LITTLE JOY IN SCHOOLS, BUT WE TRY TO MAKE THIS A JOYFUL PLACE.

I HEY, CARLOS,

'SUP, STOVE?

AND THE KIDS KNOW WE RESPECT THEM, EMPATHIZE WITH THEM, CARE ABOUT THEM, AND THAT WE'RE HERE TO TEACH.

I'M STILL TRYING TO LIVE THE STRUGGLE...

THAT'S HOW I HONOR THE HUNGER STRIKERS.

THE FOUNDING STORY IS MORE THAN A SYMBOL TO THESE TEACHERS, STUDENTS, AND PARENTS. IT'S BECOME A LIVING REFERENCE POINT FOR THINKING ABOUT EVERYTHING FROM CURRICULUM AND TEACHING TO STRUCTURE AND ORGANIZATION TO PERSONAL AND PROFESSIONAL RELATIONSHIPS.

HELLO, PARENTS. I'M BILL.

BEFORE WE TALK ABOUT YOUR KIDS AND THE WORK OF THIS CLASS, LET'S SPEND SOME TIME BUILDING IN THE BLOCK AREA.

COME ON! IT'LL BE FUN! WE'LL WORK TOGETHER IN SMALL GROUPS...

YOU MIGHT BE SURPRISED AT ALL WE LEARN FROM IT. THEN, WE'LL TALK ABOUT BLOCKS, AND, OF COURSE, YOUR CHILDREN.

LET'S ADD A BRIDGE.

HERE'S WHERE WE'LL PUT THE HELIPORT.

HOW?

8

COMMENCEMENT: BEGINNING AGAIN

THE INTELLECTUAL CHALLENGE OF TEACHING INVOLVES
BECOMING A STUDENT OF YOUR STUDENTS, UNLOCKING
THE WISDOM IN THE ROOM, AND JOINING TOGETHER ON A
JOURNEY OF DISCOVERY AND SURPRISE. THE ETHICAL
DEMAND IS TO SEE EACH STUDENT AS A 3-DIMENSIONAL
CREATURE, MUCH LIKE YOURSELF, AND AN UNSHAKABLE
FAITH IN THE IRREDUCIBLE AND INCALCULABLE VALUE OF
EVERY HUMAN BEING.

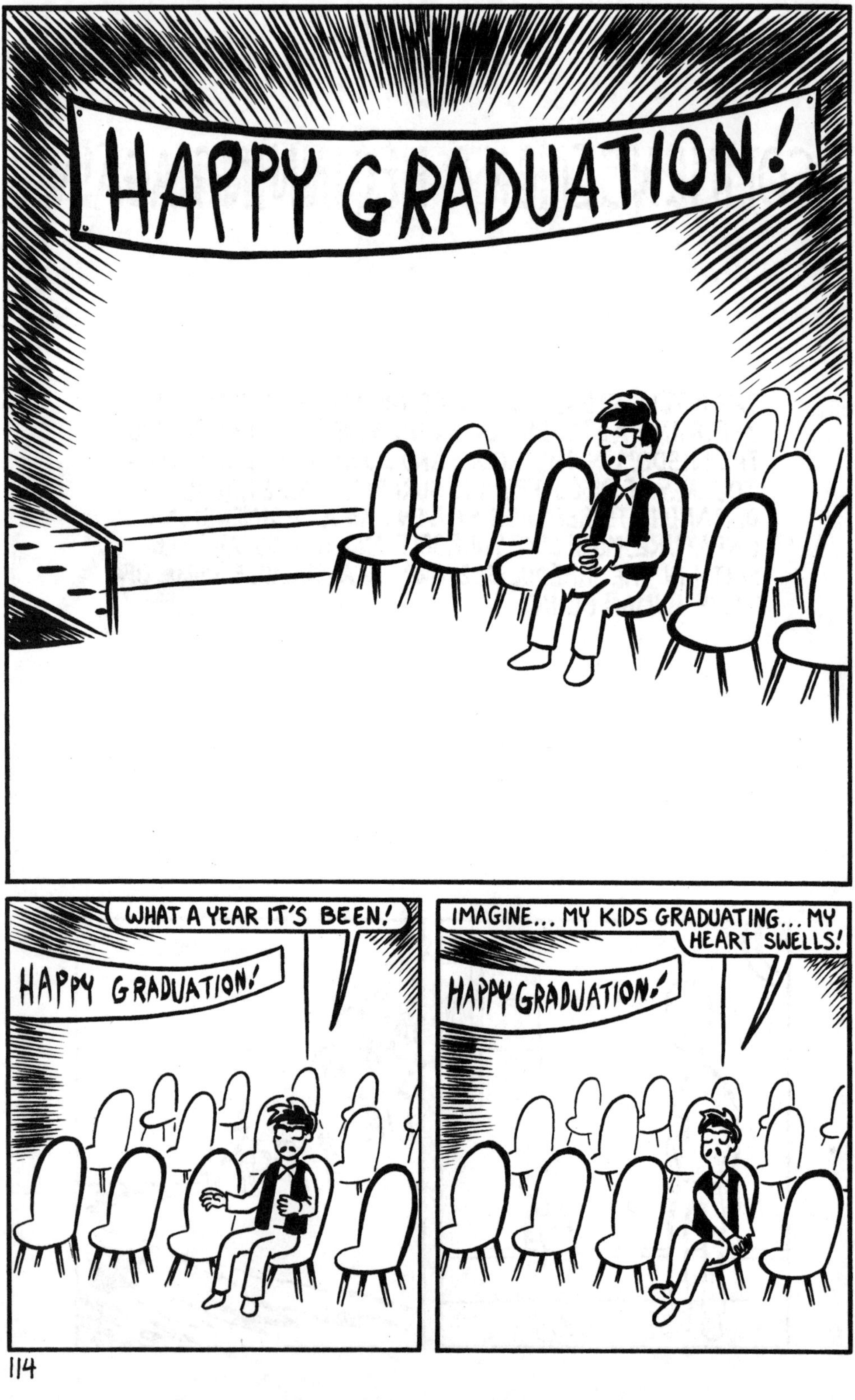
HAPPY GRADUATION!
WHAT A YEAR IT'S BEEN!
HAPPY GRADUATION!
IMAGINE... MY KIDS GRADUATING... MY HEART SWELLS!
HAPPY GRADUATION!

AND AS THE YEAR ENDS, I KNOW THAT MY JOURNEY IS JUST BEGINNING...

HAPPY GRADUATION!

I'VE LEARNED SO MUCH, BUT I KNOW THERE'S ALWAYS MORE TO DO, MORE TO LEARN.

TO TEACH IS TO ENTER INTO AN INTELLECTUAL AND ETHICAL ENTERPRISE.

IT IS TO CHOOSE A LIFE OF CHALLENGE.

BECOMING A WONDERFUL TEACHER IS A LIFETIME AFFAIR, ALWAYS QUESTIONING, ALWAYS EXPLORING, ALWAYS OPEN TO THE NEW AND THE STRANGE.

IF WE ALREADY KNOW EVERYTHING, WE ARE TERRIBLE STUDENTS AND BAD TEACHERS.

HAPPY GRADUATION!

DANG, BILL, WHY DIDN'T YOU TELL ME YOU HAD A SNACK TABLE UP IN HERE? WE COULDA BEEN HANGIN' OUT ALL YEAR.

GEEZ, RYAN, LEAVE SOME FOR THE KIDS...

YEAH, YEAH... DID I OVERHEAR YOU PONTIFICATING AGAIN?

I CAN'T STOP MYSELF!

IT'S AN ENDLESS INVESTIGATION. THE LINE BETWEEN TEACHER AND STUDENT IS SO COMPLEX AND UNCERTAIN... THESE ROLES COULD BE EXAMINED AND EXPLORED INDEFINITELY...

TOTALLY!

LIKE WHEN I VISITED PAUL'S CLASS WHEN WE FIRST STARTED THE BOOK. HE'S A TEACHER NOW...

...BUT I'LL ALWAYS REMEMBER US AS 2 KIDS GOOFING OFF IN 7TH-GRADE MATH CLASS...

PROBABILITY

...OR, ON THE LAST DAY OF MY 1ST SEMESTER TEACHING ELEMENTARY SCHOOL KIDS HOW TO DRAW COMICS, I TOOK THEM OUTSIDE FOR FREE PLAY...

FOR REAL! I REMEMBER WHEN I WAS IN 4TH GRADE, I SAW MY TEACHER AT A DEPARTMENT STORE...

WHAT ARE YOU DOING HERE? YOU'RE NOT SUPPOSED TO BE *BUYING SHOES!*

I SAW ONE OF *MY* KIDS AT A MUSIC FESTIVAL LAST YEAR...

MR. LESSING?! NO WAY!!

AND THEN SHE RAN AWAY...

I THINK THE THING YOU DON'T REALIZE UNTIL YOU'VE CROSSED OVER IS THAT TEACHERS ARE JUST REGULAR PEOPLE DOING THEIR JOBS.

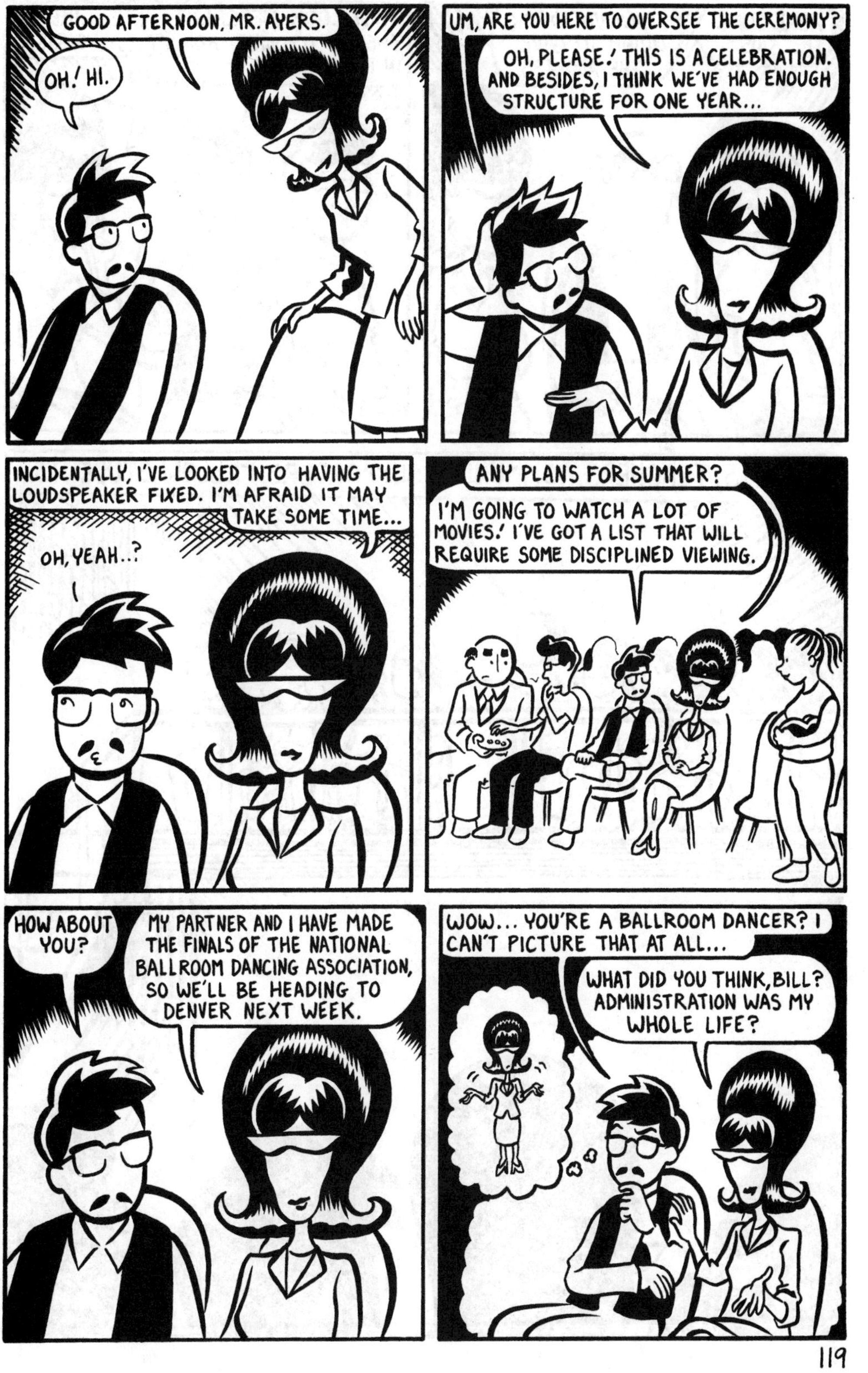
GOOD AFTERNOON, MR. AYERS.
OH! HI.
UM, ARE YOU HERE TO OVERSEE THE CEREMONY?
OH, PLEASE! THIS IS A CELEBRATION. AND BESIDES, I THINK WE'VE HAD ENOUGH STRUCTURE FOR ONE YEAR...
INCIDENTALLY, I'VE LOOKED INTO HAVING THE LOUDSPEAKER FIXED. I'M AFRAID IT MAY TAKE SOME TIME...
OH, YEAH..?
ANY PLANS FOR SUMMER?
I'M GOING TO WATCH A LOT OF MOVIES! I'VE GOT A LIST THAT WILL REQUIRE SOME DISCIPLINED VIEWING.
HOW ABOUT YOU?
MY PARTNER AND I HAVE MADE THE FINALS OF THE NATIONAL BALLROOM DANCING ASSOCIATION, SO WE'LL BE HEADING TO DENVER NEXT WEEK.
WOW... YOU'RE A BALLROOM DANCER? I CAN'T PICTURE THAT AT ALL...
WHAT DID YOU THINK, BILL? ADMINISTRATION WAS MY WHOLE LIFE?

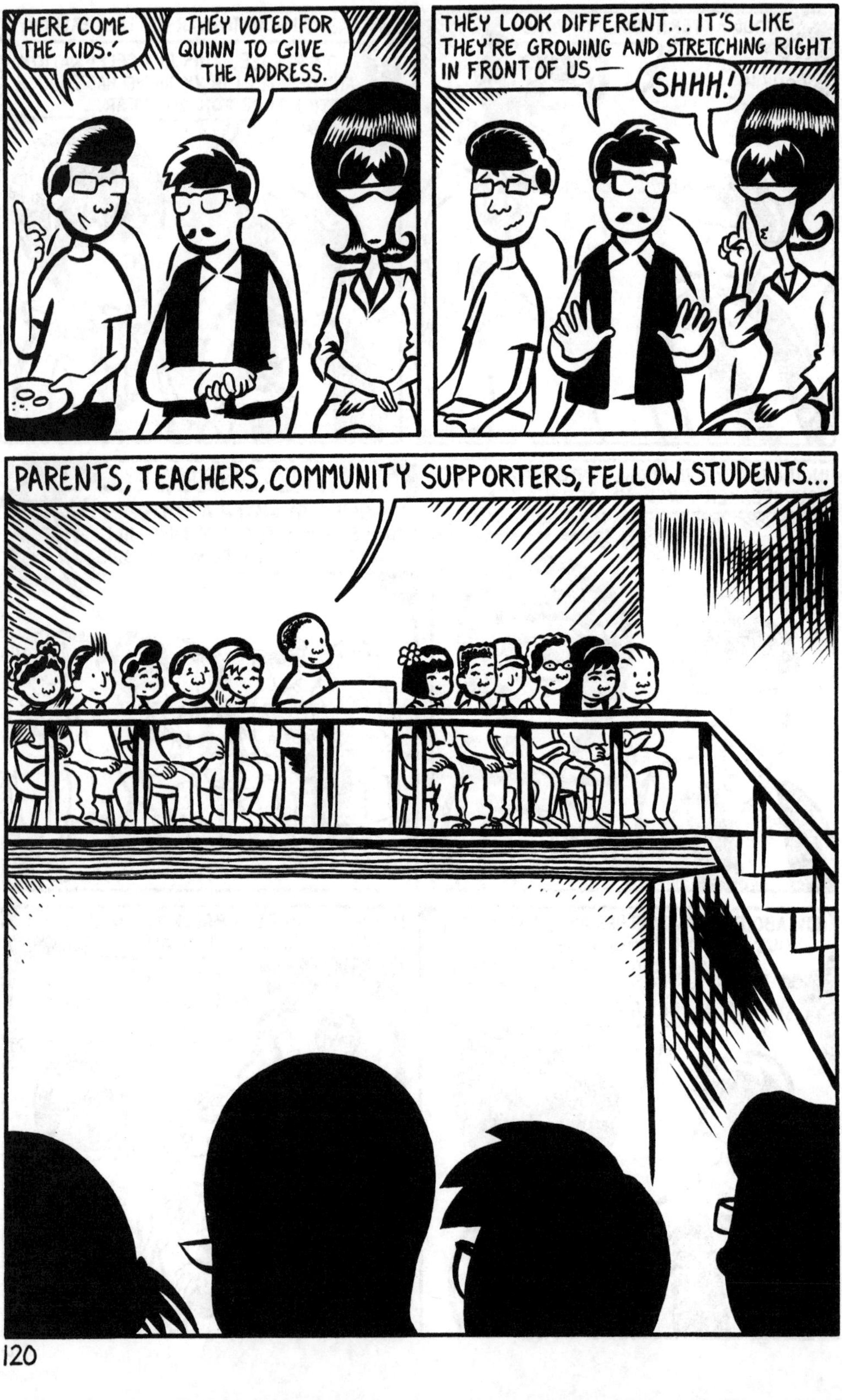
HERE COME THE KIDS.'
THEY VOTED FOR QUINN TO GIVE THE ADDRESS.
THEY LOOK DIFFERENT... IT'S LIKE THEY'RE GROWING AND STRETCHING RIGHT IN FRONT OF US —
SHHH!
PARENTS, TEACHERS, COMMUNITY SUPPORTERS, FELLOW STUDENTS...

TOGETHER WE'VE LEARNED SO MUCH, BUT THERE IS ALWAYS MORE TO KNOW AND TO BECOME.

EACH OF US IS IN TRANSITION, IN MOTION, DYNAMIC AND ON THE MOVE, WORKS-IN-PROGRESS.

AS LONG AS I LIVE I AM UNDER CONSTRUCTION.

EDUCATION AT ITS BEST RESTS ON TWIN PILLARS OF ENLIGHTENMENT AND LIBERATION.

WE'RE FREER THAN WE SOMETIMES REALIZE, BUT THAT KNOWLEDGE BEGS THE QUESTION, "GIVEN WHAT WE KNOW NOW, WHAT ARE WE GOING TO DO ABOUT IT?"

IN A DEMOCRACY, EDUCATION IS POWERED BY A BELIEF IN THE IRREDUCIBLE VALUE OF EVERY HUMAN LIFE.

WE LEARNED THAT OUR ACTIONS AS TEACHERS AND STUDENTS, AS CITIZENS AND COMMUNITY MEMBERS, ECHO DOWN THE GENERATIONS AND THAT A USEFUL GUIDE FOR ALL OF US IS TO TRY TO RESPOND TO THE DREAMS OF YOUTH.

YOU CAN CHANGE YOUR LIFE, AND TOGETHER WE CAN CHANGE THE WORLD.

TODAY QUINN IS HIMSELF A TEACHER.

HIS DAYS ARE PUNCTUATED WITH DISCOVERY AND SURPRISE...

...JOY AND CHALLENGE...

...TEACHING AND LEARNING...

WHY DOES THE WHEEL GO AROUND?

I HAVE NO IDEA!

LET'S FIGURE IT OUT TOGETHER.

123

FURTHER READINGS

ON TEACHING:

HOFFMAN, M. (2007). "*YOU WON'T REMEMBER ME": THE SCHOOLBOYS OF BARBIANA SPEAK TO TODAY.* NEW YORK: TEACHERS COLLEGE PRESS.

hooks, b. (1994). *TEACHING TO TRANSGRESS: EDUCATION AS THE PRACTICE OF FREEDOM.* NEW YORK: ROUTLEDGE.

LADSON-BILLINGS, G. (1994). *THE DREAMKEEPERS: SUCCESSFUL TEACHERS OF AFRICAN AMERICAN STUDENTS.* SAN FRANCISCO: JOSSEY-BASS.

MEIER, D. (1996). *THE POWER OF THEIR IDEAS: LESSONS FOR AMERICA FROM A SMALL SCHOOL IN HARLEM.* BOSTON: BEACON PRESS.

NIETO, S. (1996). *AFFIRMING DIVERSITY: THE SOCIOPOLITICAL CONTEXT OF MULTIRACIAL EDUCATION.* WHITE PLAINS, NY: LONGMAN.

ROSE, M. (1995). *POSSIBLE LIVES: THE PROMISE OF PUBLIC EDUCATION IN AMERICA.* BOSTON: PENGUIN.

ON COMICS:

BARRY, L. (2008). *WHAT IT IS.* MONTREAL: DRAWN AND QUARTERLY.

BRUNETTI, I. (2007). *CARTOONING PHILOSOPHY AND PRACTICE.* OAKLAND, CA: BUENAVENTURA PRESS.

McCLOUD, S. (1994). *UNDERSTANDING COMICS: THE INVISIBLE ART.* NEW YORK: HARPERCOLLINS.

WOLK, D. (2007). *READING COMICS: HOW GRAPHIC NOVELS WORK AND WHAT THEY MEAN.* PHILADELPHIA: DA CAPO PRESS.

REFERENCES

HUBBEL, S. (1988). *A BOOK OF BEES.* NEW YORK: HOUGHTON MIFFLIN.

STANISLAVSKY, K. (1936). *AN ACTOR PREPARES.* LONDON: ROUTLEDGE AND KEGAN PAUL.

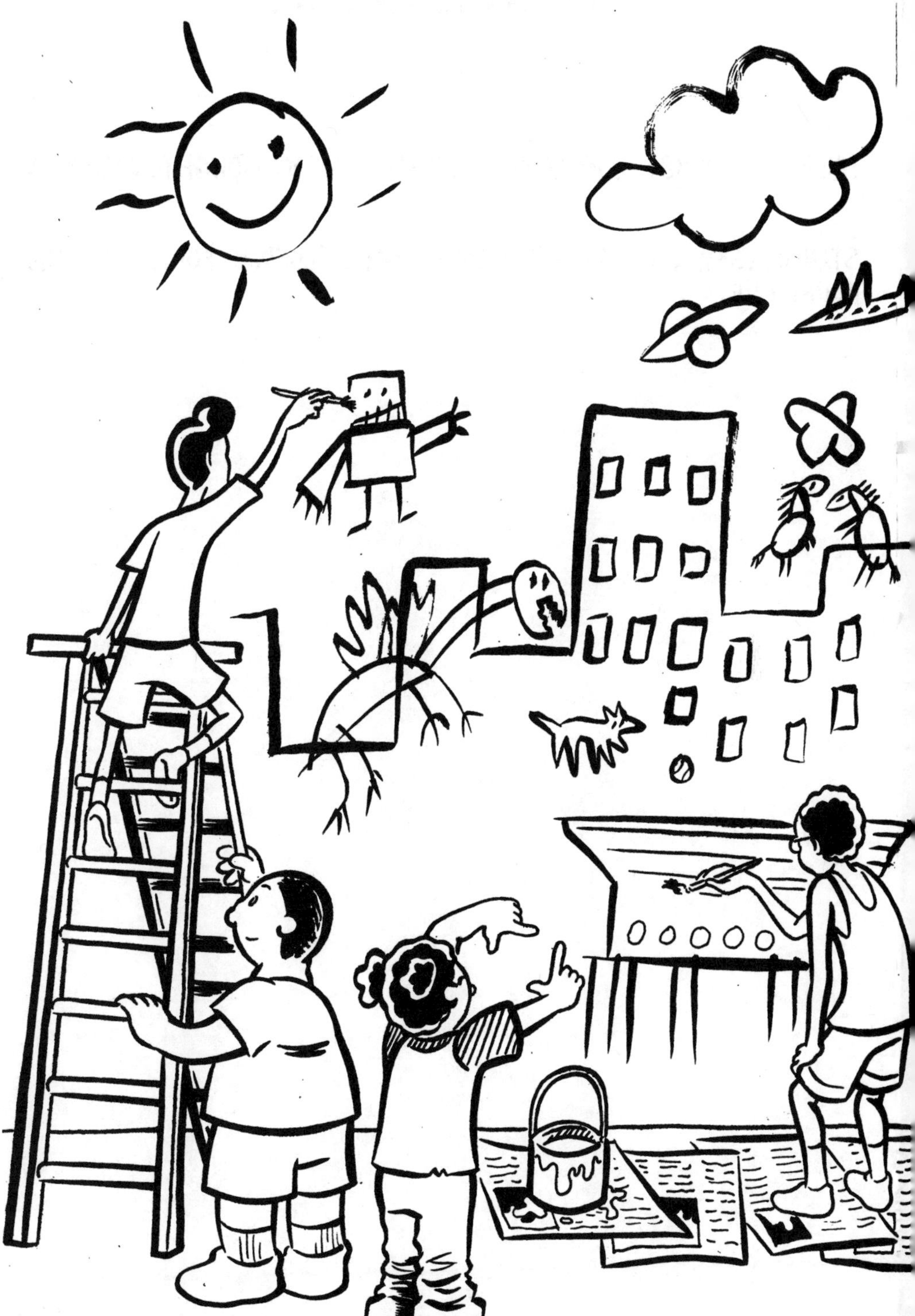

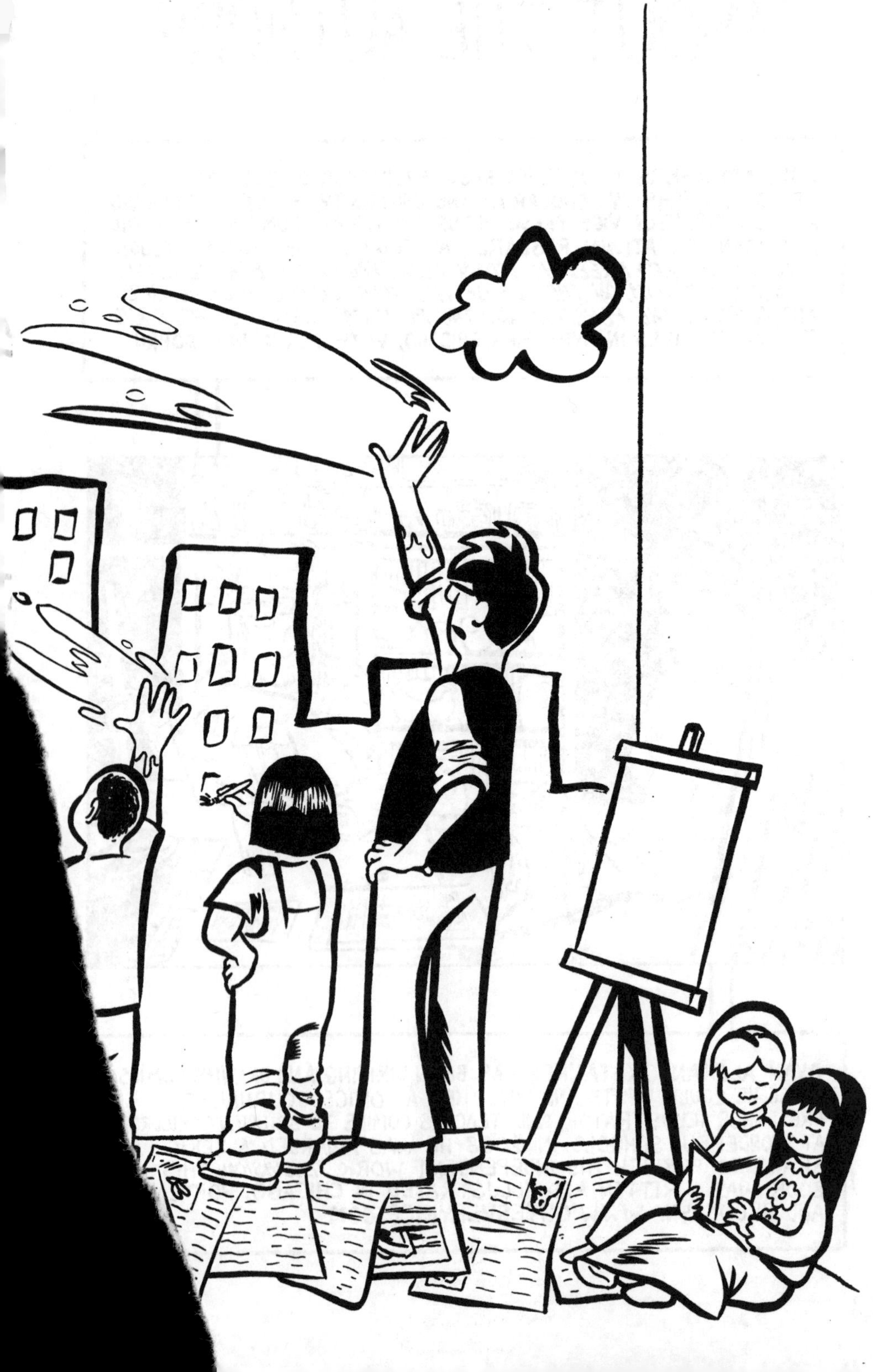

ABOUT THE AUTHORS

WILLIAM AYERS IS DISTINGUISHED PROFESSOR OF EDUCATION AND SENIOR UNIVERSITY SCHOLAR AT THE UNIVERSITY OF ILLINOIS AT CHICAGO, AND IS CURRENTLY VICE PRESIDENT OF THE CURRICULUM DIVISION OF THE AMERICAN EDUCATIONAL RESEARCH ASSOCIATION. HIS BOOKS INCLUDE *TEACHING TOWARD FREEDOM: MORAL COMMITMENT AND ETHICAL ACTION IN THE CLASSROOM, ON THE SIDE OF THE CHILD: SUMMERHILL REVISITED,* AND *TEACHING THE PERSONAL AND THE POLITICAL: ESSAYS OF HOPE AND JUSTICE.* HE LIVES IN HYDE PARK, CHICAGO, WITH BERNARDINE DOHRN.

RYAN ALEXANDER-TANNER HAS BEEN WRITING AND DRAWING COMICS SINCE HE COULD WRITE AND DRAW. HE'S A COMICS JOURNALIST, FREELANCE ILLUSTRATOR, AND TEACHES COMICS TO BRILLIANT CHILDREN AT WONDERFUL SCHOOLS. IN 2008 HE WAS AWARDED A XERIC GRANT TO PUBLISH HIS INDEPENDENT WORK, *TELEVISION.* THIS BOOK WAS WRITTEN AND ILLUSTRATED IN CHICAGO, PORTLAND AND BROOKLYN. WWW.OHYESVERYNICE.COM